I0522144

High Heels on Gravel

Tamara M. Gordon

© 2023 by Tamara M. Gordon

ALL RIGHTS RESERVED. No part of this book may be reproduced in any written, electronic, recording, or photocopying without written permission of the publisher or author. The exception would be in the case of brief quotations embodied in the critical articles or reviews and pages where permission is specifically granted by the publisher or author.

LEGAL DISCLAIMER. Although the author has made every effort to ensure that the information in this book was correct at press time, the author do not assume and hereby disclaim any liability to any party for any loss, damage, or disruption caused by errors or omissions, whether such errors or omissions result from negligence, accident, or any other cause.

Bible Scriptures From Various Versions of The Bible

Library of Congress Cataloging – in- Publication Data has been applied for.

Paperback ISBN: 979-8-9891638-6-1

PRINTED IN THE UNITED STATES OF AMERICA.

Book Publishing Services by Pen Legacy LLC. (www.penlegacy.com)

FIRST EDITION

Table of Content

High Heels on Gravel

Foreword

Have you ever needed a girlfriend you could talk to about anything? A girlfriend who not only talked the talk but walked the walk? One who does not always tell you what you want to hear but what you NEED to hear for your good? A girlfriend who instills wisdom, knowledge, and understanding whenever you are seeking it? A girlfriend who gives it to you like it truly 'tis—the good, bad, and definitely the ugly. God knew exactly what I needed when He allowed me to be Tamara's mother. I just had to wait until a time of maturity. Over the years, I have watched her blossom into the woman she is today. She's the one with not a hair out of place. Her wardrobe is always impeccable, and her makeup flawless. She commands the attention of everyone in a room when she enters, whether it's the living room or the boardroom. When she speaks, her conversations are always of value and even sprinkled with a scripture or two. She's very witty, and I have taken pride in the fact that we can learn from one another.

Using the lessons learned on this road called life, Tamara has mastered how to inspire and encourage those seeking direction on topics most people feel are taboo. She was raised in the church but is unapologetic about who she is, and I love that for her. I drew her before she was born, and she is eerily like the picture. Even with her magnetic personality, she is extremely humble. I still marvel at how people receive her. Albeit guarded, she is a woman with a heart of gold. You, the readers, will be shocked as she shares her firsthand account of loving people through incarceration and even addiction. No, she doesn't look like what she has been through!

The part of my daughter YOU don't see is that while she is sporting her trendy heels, her feet sometimes hurt. Hurt in the sense of dealing with life. Still, she continues on the journey, making it her own. Psalm 23 is a scripture I've always shared with her—*"Ye though I walk through..."* I've witnessed my daughter sacrifice herself, internalize many emotions, take things for "the team" on several occasions, and fight back tears she desperately tried to hide from me and others. Being her mother, I sometimes wanted to intercede and shelter her, but I admire how she continues to press her way to the mark of the high calling in Jesus. The road of life is not always smooth, and oftentimes, she has traveled alone on her road, but *we know ALL things work together for good to them that love God—Romans 8:28.*

With all Tamara endures to achieve her persona and devotion to her family, friends, and craft, the unseen portion of her making exposed in this devotional is like *High Heels on Gravel.* I pray her revelations help you to open your eyes and heart to God's Word in a whole new way. I'm certain you will enjoy it!

Tamara's Mom,

Denise E. Manning

We Plan, God Laughs

James 4:15
For that ye ought to say, If the Lord will, we shall live, and do this, or that.

Proverbs 16:3
Commit your work to the LORD, and your plans will be established.

Jeremiah 29:11
For I know the plans I have for you, declares the LORD, plans for welfare and not for evil, to give you a future and a hope.

"Plan well. Prepare diligently. Pray hard. Then, go for it with your whole heart."

~ Charles R. Swindoll

Tamara M. Gordon

*A*s a young girl, life was just being lived. I was not concerned about how much it would take to become the woman I am still becoming. Yet, even with the mindset of living in the moment, I learned that some things are out of my control. While in grammar school, I was encouraged by a 6th-grade teacher to start planning for my future. Of course, back then, I did not fully understand the magnitude of this advice. So, naturally, I operated in the "today" — living life one day at a time and not worrying about tomorrow. That teacher's statement soon came back to haunt me as I was promoted to the 10th grade and faced having to plan for my immediate future. *The future. There goes that word again,* I thought to myself, but I took it to heart this time. I distinctly recall mulling over my future in great detail, creating a checklist, and planning my life for the decades to come. Looking back now, I have to admit I am so grateful that God saw fit to change some things, add some things, delay some things, and deny me of some things.

We should all do our due diligence by making plans for our lives, but we must also allow God to move on our behalf. The book of James explains how important it is to leave our personal ego and arrogance out of the equation. Everything is in accordance and driven by the will of God, and we cannot go wrong consulting with God before making our plans. After all, He wants us to trust and depend on Him fully. So, of course, we should make plans. However, we must understand that none of them will be successful if they are not in God's will! Do not let your arrogance masked as diligence fool you. God is in control!

As you go about your day today, work on consistently including God in the making of your plans. He's on your side and wants you to be victorious.

Do you have specific plans for your life that you need God to intervene? Write down your goal(s) and some action items you will do to ensure greater success.

_____

_____

_____

_____

_____

_____

_____

_____

_____

_____

_____

_____

_____

_____

_____

_____

_____

Tamara M. Gordon

_____

_____

_____

_____

_____

_____

_____

_____

_____

_____

_____

_____

_____

_____

_____

_____

_____

_____

_____

_____

Prayer

Lord, thank you for another chance to serve you. Only you know my end from the beginning, and you have figured out every detail in between. I am grateful you know me because you made me, and nothing I do or say catches you off guard. You know what I want to do and the goals and plans of my heart, but Father, I want your will to be done. If I am on the wrong path, Father, give me direction and strength to accept and follow your lead. May every decision I make be pleasing to you as I lay every plan at your feet. In Jesus' name, I believe and pray. Amen.

Do It Scared

Psalm 56:3

When I am afraid, I put my trust in you.

Psalm 34:4

I sought the LORD, and he heard me, and delivered me from all my fears.

Proverbs 29:25

The fear of man brings a snare: but whoever puts his trust in the LORD shall be safe.

Exodus 14:14

The Lord shall fight for you, and ye shall hold your peace.

Deuteronomy 20:4

For the Lord, your God is he that goeth with you, to fight for you against your enemies, to save you.

Tamara M. Gordon

*E*very summer, my family would wake up before the
break of day, pack up the car, and head out to spend
all day at Punderson State Park. Usually, we were one
of the first families there, and all the kids would eagerly
make our way down to what we called the beach, although I
am not sure it qualified as one. I would inch further and
further away from the picnic site with everyone else and
celebrate my success when my mother did not summon me
back. The kids would run into the water, taking on the waves
and playing water games. I immediately lost my excitement
because the only thing to do at the "beach" was swim, and I
didn't know how. I told myself that I would learn to swim so
I could join my comrades next summer. However, year after
year, I let my fear get the best of me. You probably think I
eventually got over being deathly afraid of learning to swim,
but you would be wrong. I recognize today that my fear kept
me from enjoying activities as a child and a young adult. For
the longest, my fear of swimming was based on "what ifs"
and consumed my thinking with the worst scenarios.

Fear is one of the most common weapons the enemy uses
to shortchange us from achieving our goals, big and small. I
am not suggesting you will never be anxious or afraid
because I do not believe that to be practical. But what I am
telling you is that God has a way of removing doubt, calming
fears, and helping us through whatever it is we are facing.
So, while it is most likely I will never make it back to
Punderson State Park to conquer that body of water, you can
rest assured that whatever sand my feet land on, I will have
more than a picture opportunity in the water. There is
nothing wrong with letting the Lord know you are afraid. In
the book of Psalms, King David makes this confession several
times! *(See Psalm 34:4; Psalm 55:4-5.)* His confessions were

often wrapped in prayer, acknowledging the Lord's power over his fears and enemies. These are examples we can follow.

In the biblical narrative of the Books of Samuel, David— a young shepherd and harpist from humble beginnings— gains his clout by killing the giant Goliath with only a slingshot. He becomes a favorite of Saul, the first king of Israel, but that is short-lived once Saul becomes paranoid and insecure, believing that David is trying to take his throne. According to the Bible, David is writing after the Philistines had captured him in Gath. He calls on the Lord because he is afraid and desperate. As always, God showed up and spared the life of David. Psalm 56 was David's prayer in Gath when the block got too hot. Without a doubt, David was scared to death when he was in Philistine city, but he remembered God's promises and the Lord's call on his life. Long story short, David returned to his land and became King of Israel. It wasn't easy; it wasn't without battle, and it wasn't even without doubt. The lesson is simply that no matter how we feel or how afraid we may be, God can and will make it happen for us. This stirred up my interest in learning to swim.

Years later, I found enough courage to graduate from just getting in the water to actually swimming. And while I am no Simone Manuel (the first Black woman to win an individual Olympic gold medal) or Maritza Correia (the first record-setting Black swimmer) out here on the water, I can do more than look like a wader when cruising, visiting pools, or vacationing on the ocean. I can do what the culture refers to as "save myself." I'm good with that because, ultimately, that is the goal!

So, ask yourself if you see "giants" in life through the eyes of God or your own human eyesight. There is no shame in admitting you fear water, heights, criticism, failure, or even success. In fact, David called on the Lord in various situations. Don't you dare fear any giant. When you have God on your side, you can face it and have victory, just like David.

Is there something you have always wanted to do, but fear or anxiety has held you back?

_____

_____

_____

_____

_____

_____

_____

_____

_____

_____

_____

_____

_____

Name a "giant" and what you will do to fight it and win.

_____

_____

_____

_____

_____

_____

_____

_____

_____

_____

_____

_____

_____

_____

_____

_____

_____

Tamara M. Gordon

Prayer

Father, thank you for not sending me into any battle alone. Thank you for having my back in everything I do and protecting me from my enemies and fears. I ask that you strike down all the giants that may come against me, Lord, and lead me to victory. No matter how large my battles are today, help me to understand that they are not mine but yours. You are strong and mighty in battle and cannot lose a fight. Lord, go before me in all that I do so the world will see that greater is He that is in me. In Jesus' name, Amen.

Friends...
How Many of Us Have Them

Ecclesiastes 4:9-12

Two people are better off than one, for they can help each other succeed. If one person falls, the other can reach out and help. But someone who falls alone is in real trouble. Likewise, two people lying close together can keep each other warm. But how can one be warm alone? A person standing alone can be attacked and defeated, but two can stand back-to-back and conquer.

Ecclesiastes 4:9-12

Three are even better, for a triple-braided cord is not easily broken.

Psalm 101:6

I will search for faithful people to be my companions.

Tamara M. Gordon

Friends is a word we use every day.
Most the time we use it in the wrong way.
Now you can look the word up, again and again.
But the dictionary doesn't know the meaning of friends.

~ Whodini

*U*nfortunately, most of us know far too well the sting of pain inflicted by a friend. Always considered the popular girl, I easily attracted people who wanted to be around me. Discerning if they were good to be around was a different ballgame. At various stages in my life, I had an assigned BFF, and in that season, I probably never considered how hard the "forever" would be. Needless to say, after several proclamations of friendships here and there, none endured the test of time. Everything from mixed motives, unilateral care, and "growing apart" could be cited for their termination. Having repeated this cycle through high school, college, and young adulthood, I became jaded by the thought of having a best friend—much less one that would be around forever.

When I was younger, my qualifiers for a female BFF were anything from jumping double-dutch and talking about boys to playing basketball and shopping. As time went on and I grew older, I learned that most of these friendships were not meant to last a lifetime. My defense mechanism was to tell myself I didn't need friends, but God began to show me the error in my thinking.

In my late 20s, I began being intentional in my friendship journeys and recognizing everyone needs them. Far from being the little girl who couldn't identify her needs from others, I can honestly say that I thank God for my squad of girlfriends who are authentic, honest, available, and reciprocal as grown women. These friendships are what I wanted and needed thirty-five years ago. In Ecclesiastes 4:9, King Solomon weighs in on the benefit of friendships in every aspect of life. Two are indeed better than one in labor when we are weak or ill, in combat or competition, and even for basic survival. In these proverbs, the illustration of a man falling in a ditch showed that a friend was needed to get himself out.

God created relationships at the start of the world. There is emphasis that He must also be in the mix of who we call a friend in order for that union to be successful and good for us. The image is explained in Ecclesiastes 4:12, "A cord of three strands is not quickly broken." The three-strand cord is understood to be unity between yourself, God, and another person. David discussed his prerequisites for choosing friends in Psalm 101 and sums up his criteria thus: the most important characteristic to look for is faithfulness.

God designed all relationships—including friendships—to help fill the gaps in our lives. He demonstrates the importance and benefits of a good friend throughout the Bible in the story of David and Jonathon, Naomi and Ruth, and the ultimate with humanity and Christ. I have been blessed to find my circle of true friendships, and I thank God for them. I pray the same for you!

Tamara M. Gordon

Think about a simple way you can be a better friend. How will you intentionally go about doing that?

_____

_____

_____

_____

_____

_____

_____

_____

_____

_____

_____

_____

_____

_____

_____

_____

_____

Prayer

Father, thank you for covering me as my ultimate friend. Thank you for showing me what true friends look like. Lord, I am asking you to look into my friendships and show me if there is one who is not a true friend. Help me also to look at myself to make sure I am being the friend they need me to be. Increase our circle in love, support, and faithfulness so that we can continue to bear the burdens of one another and make each one of us better. Grant me and my friends favor and continue to place godly people in our lives so that we will continue to be blessed. In Jesus' name, Amen.

No Rest for the Weary

Philippians 4:6-7
Do not be anxious about anything, but in everything, by prayer and petition, with thanksgiving, present your requests to God. And the peace of God, which transcends all understanding, will guard your hearts and minds in Christ Jesus.

Psalm 23:1-2
The Lord is my shepherd, I lack nothing. He makes me lie down in green pastures; he leads me beside quiet waters.

I have spent the greater part of the last decade of my life fighting to go to sleep and stay asleep but to no avail. I tried everything from changing my diet, exercise routine, and medication. Still, there was no rest. Needless to say, this impacted my productivity and attitude the following day, and this soon became a part of my "normal life." Even in the midst of this, I knew there was no normalcy in working long hours, wearing multiple hats, and not getting enough rest. This just couldn't be my life. Crash and burn, crash and burn—year after year. My aging body began to take a physical hit with not getting enough rest. After speaking to a professional, I learned I was unable to rest because I would not allow my overthinking mind to settle down. I was taking my daily stresses and anxiety about self, family, work life, extracurricular activities, and parenting to bed with me every night. Again, crash and burn. The stress of this thing we call "life" can and will keep you up at night. Worldly pressures and problems will rob you of your peace if you are not careful. Carrying the weight for years did not end well for me. I found myself physically, emotionally, mentally, and spiritually ill with no "cure" in sight.

In this passage, Paul is writing to the Christians in Philippi. Paul reminds the saints about God's presence and His power. He implored them—and us—not to allow fear, anxiety, or stress to break our rest. Have confidence in knowing that whatever is still on your plate when you lie down is no match for the Lord. As we all know, our bodies cannot produce, heal, or function without rest. In those anxious moments, when you cannot find peace to rest, turn to Jesus. Living under constant stress is not God's will for your life. Instead, give Him all your worries all the time so you can get some rest. Some real rest!

What are your stressors in life?

_____

_____

_____

_____

_____

_____

_____

_____

_____

_____

_____

_____

_____

_____

_____

_____

_____

Tamara M. Gordon

How do you deal with anxiety and stress?

_____

_____

_____

_____

_____

_____

_____

_____

_____

_____

_____

_____

_____

_____

_____

_____

_____

_____

Prayer

Lord, you know I am tired and feeling anxious. I trust you to calm all my fears and bring about your peace that will surpass my understanding. Amen.

Meeting People Where They Are

1 Peter 3:9

Do not repay evil with evil or insult with insult. On the contrary, repay evil with blessing, because to this you were called so that you may inherit a blessing.

Proverbs 15:1

A soft answer turns away wrath, but a harsh word stirs up anger.

Just so we are clear, salvation is indeed free, but this Christian journey will test everything in you. Most days, I find it small work to do the right thing. I do this by asking myself, "What Would Jesus Do?" However, every now and then, somebody will catch me with my Jesus odometer on "five miles 'til empty". It is those times when my humanity is closer to "try me" than "hallelujah"! I'm not exactly proud to admit this, but everybody gets tired of taking the high road at some point or another.

Years ago, I told myself I would no longer allow people to take me out of character. I had made the decision to take the high road with everything and everybody. In that moment, me, myself, and I laughed because I knew for certain my patience with people would be challenged. On this particular day, we encountered many people during our trip to the mall who displayed poor customer service or rude behavior, but I refrained from responding. You would have to know the old me to understand how much of an undertaking it was to let it slide. However, my restraint came to an end while in a department store. I don't want to misconstrue the facts, but what I do remember is the employee mumbling, "You people," under her breath as she walked away from the cash register. While everybody else decided to ignore her comment, I just could not.

Before I knew it, I found myself responding and not with the image of Jesus in mind. Hindsight is 20/20, and even with the maturity and discipline I have acquired, I still fall short on some days. Not intentionally, but hey, I'm human, just like everyone else walking this earth. Nobody is perfect, not even your pastor.

In the text 1st Peter 3:9, Peter makes it plain how Christians should respond to evil. For Christians, revenge or battle is never the right answer. Peter writes to people who are experiencing both verbal and physical attacks for following Christ. He stressed the need for empathy and compassion, even for non-believers. We are further obliged to bless those who operate in evil so that we will be the inheritor of a blessing for ourselves. This passage is often used when speaking to wives regarding submitting to their husbands, but we all can learn a lesson on how to submit to doing things the Christ way. In this case, the godly way would have been for me to respond with a soft tongue or not at all. I failed then, but I will not when tested the next time!

Have a moment of honesty with yourself. Think about the difference in how you would have responded ten years ago and how you would respond today. How far have you come? What do you still need to work on?

_____

_____

_____

_____

_____

_____

_____

_____

_____

_____

_____

_____

_____

Tamara M. Gordon

Prayer

Father God, thank you for giving me a new day to get it right. Lord, please guide me and give me the discernment to hear your voice in every situation I encounter. Help me to see things not meant for my good and to respond right, even when people treat me wrong. Help me to overcome adversities and give me the strength and courage to walk away. Finally, work on my pride so I do not feel the need to have the final say. In your name, I pray. Amen.

Feeling Some Kinda Way

Psalm 34:17-18
When the righteous cry for help, the Lord hears and delivers them out of all their troubles. The Lord is near to the brokenhearted and saves the crushed in spirit."

Deuteronomy 31:8
The Lord himself goes before you and will be with you; he will never leave you nor forsake you. Do not be afraid; do not be discouraged.

*"Depression is the common cold of our emotions.
Eventually it touches everyone—even God's people."*
                                                    (Anonymous)

I hate being cold and have never been too fond of winters in the Midwest. The subfreezing temperatures, coupled with the inches of snow, never helped my mood, and as I grew older, I began to notice some specific things that correlated to wintertime. I noticed that my mood was never the best during this season, and I was even less productive while trying to balance my professional life, family, friends, and all the extracurricular activities on my plate. I'm sure this change in me became more evident over the years, as much from the outside as it was on the inside.

When I tell you it was *bad*, it was just that—so much so that I spoke to my primary care physician about it during a standard appointment. Imagine my surprise when she replied, "Sounds like you have a case of seasonal affective disorder." After a few moments of awkward silence, I asked her to explain this to me, and she summed it up as "winter depression." It did not go unnoticed by me how the original diagnosis transitioned from an official medical word to a simpler term; I am certain it was due to my initial expression to her comment. To any extent, it was at that moment I realized I had an incorrect understanding of what depression looked like and who it could affect. Since knowing is half the battle, I started putting things into place to overcome this "disorder". I did everything from changing my eating habits to strictly enforcing my self-care routine during winter months, just to name a couple. Though not always easy to do, when consistent and intentional, these things help!

Depression showed up in the prophet Elijah in the Old Testament. Elijah lived and served during the days of the wicked king, Ahab, and his queen, Jezebel, who introduced Baal worship in Israel. Chosen by God, Elijah challenged the king and the prophets of Baal in his mission to call the nation back from apostasy. Suffice it to say Elijah won that bloody fight on Mt. Carmel, proving to Israel that Jehovah was the Lord. But after that victory, the queen sent a death threat to Elijah! Overcome with fear, Elijah left everything behind and disappeared into the wilderness, where he sat under a tree praying, fearing he would die. While he slept, an angel woke him up multiple times to provide food and drink, but Elijah would go back to sleep. Eventually, the angel told him to go on a journey to Mt. Horeb. When Elijah got there, he spent the night in a cave where he complained about his situation while relishing his pity party.

I cannot look down on Elijah because we have all had those moments where we feel we have given our best to a situation, family, friend, or even a cause and have not received the same in return. Through the experience of Elijah, God shows us how easy it is to be up one day and down another. Some of us may need time away from everything to refuel our mind, body, and soul. If we do not, we will surely burn out, stress out, or fall into depression.

As Christians, we are not exempt from moments of anxiety and depression, but just like God restored Elijah at his lowest, He will do the same for each of us. From this day forward, we will recognize that our mental, physical, and spiritual body is a priority and will handle ourselves with care. When you find yourself having an Elijah moment, take time to say the prayer that follows:

Prayer

Father God, please help me to be as good to myself as I am to others. Give me the strength to free my mind from thoughts of fear, failure, and futility. Help me to trust and know that you will always come through. Amen.

Teamwork Makes The Dream Work

Ephesians 4:16
From whom the whole body, joined and held together by every joint with which it is equipped, when each part is working properly, makes the body grow so that it builds itself up in love.

1 Corinthians 12:12
For just as the body is one and yet has many parts, and all the parts, though many, form [only] one body, so it is with Christ.

1 Peter 4:8-10
Love each other deeply because love covers a multitude of sins. Offer hospitality to one another without grumbling. Each of you should use whatever gift you have received to serve others, as faithful stewards of God's grace in its various forms.

Tamara M. Gordon

*I*f you are somebody who feels you can do it all alone and never needs any support or help from others, you, my friend, are sadly mistaken. Some of us have had the unfortunate opportunity of learning this earlier than others. Should we have personal goals? Sure! However, we should not be haughty enough to believe we can accomplish everything on our own.

I recall the day I was introduced to the game of basketball. This experience taught me a lot of things, but this story is about teamwork. I was in the 7th grade and one of two Black girls in a demographic of affluent children who wanted for nothing. My mother and I laugh about it today because we know only Jesus helped my parents pay that steep college tuition. Anyway, as I was leaving the "dining hall" where we ate meals that made fine dining look unworthy, a cheerful lady approached me in the hallway with a full stride. I happened to be walking with the only other Black girl in my class, so we stopped at her request to chat with us. Without hesitation, she asked us to come to the gymnasium after school so we could try out for the basketball team. Now, let it be known that my experience with basketball prior to that was limited to me being mad at Jordan and the Chicago Bulls for breaking the heart of the Cleveland Cavaliers, but we told her we would come.

When we got to the gymnasium after school, we were greeted with a happy face we could not interpret. We dressed and made our way to the sidelines, where we watched the coach demonstrate standard basketball moves foreign to us girls. It wasn't long before she called out, "Manning!" Of course, I responded. I remember whispering, "What are we doing," to which she sternly replied, "All I need you to do is keep your eyes on the ball and your hands up. Don't worry about anything else. THAT is your job." It then clicked that my team was on defense, and we began to consistently control the practice by doing our part. I wasn't worried about the other players' jobs, just my own, and TOGETHER, we went on to be successful.

When Nehemiah was working with the people of Jerusalem to rebuild the wall around the city, enemies of the Israelites did all they could to distract them and destroy their progress. Nehemiah was adamant and faithful to do his part to get the wall built. The Israelites had people working on the wall's foundation, while the others were guards over the builders. Just as then, some things can only be accomplished with teamwork. There may be a time in your life when you are unfamiliar with what is being asked of you, and that is okay. Be obedient, play your part, and watch God pull it all together. Bottom line is God doesn't expect us to know it all. He only expects us to do our part for the greater good.

Think about something where teamwork is essential. What position do you play, and how can you play it better so the good of the team prevails?

_____

_____

_____

_____

_____

_____

Tamara M. Gordon

Prayer

Father God, I come to you asking you to help me be the best version of myself so I can give my best to others. Please give me the discernment to understand and meet the needs of those I encounter and work with. Show me how to be a good team player to accomplish your purpose. Direct my efforts so that I may always do what leads to peace and building others up. All these things I ask in Jesus' name. Amen.

Girl, Let It Go!

Proverbs 3:5

Trust in the LORD with all your heart and lean not on your own understanding.

Isaiah 43:18-19

Forget the former things; do not dwell on the past. See, I am doing a new thing! Now it springs up; do you not perceive it? I am making a way in the wilderness and streams in the wasteland.

My favorite season is autumn. In Ohio, the long roads of trees dressed in orange, red, and yellow hues are strikingly beautiful during this time of year. And although the foliage is short-lived, the lessons we can learn from it are life-changing. The effortless process of leaves turning gorgeous shades of autumn colors is a sign that they are dying and about to fall to the ground. The good news, however, is that this cycle repeats itself as long as the tree is full of life.

Tamara M. Gordon

As women, we become good at juggling a million things but struggle with the simple act of letting go. I have had this difficult conversation with myself and can never come up with a rational explanation for why I struggle with letting things go. Maybe it is the fixer in me or being the over-understanding type, but I am learning to let it go! It is extremely exhausting trying to hold it all together with full hands. Even when weary and weak, we wrestle with holding on to everything, even if it means us no good.

Trust me when I tell you that I am guilty of holding on to some people, places, and things for far too long, and I thank God as I manage every day to let things go that no longer serve me. Despite having heard the phrase "Let go and let God" for much of my life, I never took the time to understand what it actually meant. Then, one day, it finally hit me, and ir became clear that I was going to have to do some major work on myself. I had to learn to let go of the past—things that hurt me, things that triggered me, and things I couldn't control. I would tell myself to give it to God but never remove my hands. Needless to say, playing a winless game of tug-of-war with God only makes one tired and broken. We all have things in our lives right now that may be disturbing our peace and keeping us up at night. We have things we hope will prayerfully turn around. But worrying and our inability to let go is only to our physical detriment. Sure, it will be hard, but we must learn to let go of the hurt. Quit that job, avoid conflict, walk away from that unfulfilling relationship and everything else that is not for our good. God is straight up when He says to cast our cares on Him because He cares for us." (1 Peter 5:7) He admonishes us not to be anxious about anything. Why? Because He is in complete control and does not need our help.

Think of it this way: when our hands are filled with all kinds of stuff, they cannot receive anything. Aren't you ready to release some things so your hands can be open to receive the many blessings God has promised? Listen, I know it hurts, and I know it's hard. But it's time. LET IT GO!

When you find yourself in situations that you feel are too hard to give to God, read the following lyrics by DeWayne Woods from his song titled "Let Go" as a reminder:

As soon as I stop worrying
Worrying how the story ends
I let go and I let God
Let God have His way

That's when things start happening
When I stopped looking at back then
I let go and I let God
Let God have His way

Stop Running Yo' Mouth!

Proverbs 21:23
Whoever guards his mouth and tongue keeps his soul from troubles.

Proverbs 17:27-28
He who has knowledge spares his words, And a man of understanding is of a calm spirit. Even a fool is counted wise when he holds his peace; When he shuts his lips, he is considered perceptive.

*A*s a teenager, I thought talking on the phone was the next best thing to breathing. You couldn't tell me nothing since I had a phone in my bedroom. I would wake up on the phone and ultimately fall asleep on the phone while listening to the low rhythmic breathing of somebody's son on the other end of the line. My mother would always know when I was speaking to one boy in particular because my tone and volume would change and echo throughout the house. She happened to like this guy. One day, when she had enough, she yelled to me, "If you don't have anything nice to say to him, hang *MY* phone up!" Emphasis on the "my" because she did not care that it was in my room. She paid the bill, and therefore, it was *HER* phone. As a teen, I could not understand why it was a big deal to her, and honestly, the embarrassment wouldn't let me. However, as I grew up, she explained to me that knowing how to talk and, more importantly, *when* to talk will help me in life.

I didn't get the lesson right away and continued to take a few lumps on the head for not knowing when to be quiet. I had to learn that every action did not require my reaction, and every statement did not require my response. It was not easy, and I have had more than my fair share of learned opportunities. I used to feel a need to speak my peace, clear my name, and put people in their place. But, once I learned the value of silence, my life changed for the better. The Bible suggests a few good reasons to be quiet:

- Obedience
- Self-Control
- Wisdom
- Rest

As adults, we should make valiant efforts to both the value of words and silence. It has been said that "He who has learned to hold his tongue is a greater conqueror than the warrior who subdues an empire!" I know, I know. You want to set the record straight and clear your name, but that is not always your job. Psalm 62:5 tells us, "My soul, wait in silence for God alone, for my expectation is from him." I don't know about you, but I fully expect God to show up on my behalf, and when He does, He shows out!

Meditate on the song *"Peace be Still"* by James Cleveland and write down a few things you will work to do when you want to speak but know it is best you remain silent.

Prayer

Lord, teach me to be still and quiet in you. Help me to remember that the earth is yours and the fullness thereof. Help me to be slow to speak in times of unrest and to remain comfortable with allowing you to have the last word in my life. Teach me to wait on you and be of good courage. Show up on my behalf and be my spokesperson when I am confused, persecuted, hurt, and want to complain. Keep control over my mouth so nothing comes out that is not uplifting and edifying. May the words of my mouth and meditation of my heart be acceptable to you, oh Lord, my strength and my redeemer. Amen!

Easier Said Than Done

Colossians 3:12
Put on then, as God's chosen ones, holy and beloved, compassionate hearts, kindness, humility, meekness, and patience,"

Hebrews 4:16
Let us then with confidence draw near to the throne of grace, that we may receive mercy and find grace to help in time of need.

Your grace and mercy brought me through
I'm living this moment because of You
I want to thank You and praise You, too
Your grace and mercy brought me through
~ Mississippi Mass Choir

*I*n a world that tells us, "Go hard. Be better. You can do much more than that. Hustle, and then hustle harder," it is easy to find yourself under constant pressure. This pressure may come from family, employers, institutions, peers, organizations, and even ourselves. If you are like me and many other women, you are your worst critic. Learning to be easy on the woman in the mirror is difficult yet necessary. If you are a day over 8, and maybe even younger, you understand what can happen when pressure adds up. When we feel pressured, the nervous system instructs our bodies to release stress hormones to help us cope with the imminent threats during that time. All of us have experienced this and have a stress response or "fight-or-flight" reaction. Eventually, you will hit a breaking point. This usually results in women bailing out on their hopes, dreams, and goals. We become tired of the unrealistic expectations and upset at how everything is going in life.

I cannot tell you how many times I have said aloud to friends and even myself that I have to get my life together, put myself first, or, my favorite, take care of me. Yet, I never do it. It's crazy! It is like a never-ending cycle of "I'm tired; I have to change; I'm going to do it," and back to "I'm tired." This turns into feelings of disappointment and guilt. Mind you, all of this is happening as we continue to be superwoman to the world but a villian to ourselves. Grace has many different connotations depending upon the context, but for the sake of this peace, it is simply the ability to be kind, forgiving, and gentle to ourselves. Period! This may come as a surprise to you, but as we go through anxiety, depression, being overworked, exhaustion, hormones, illness, and everything else life can and will throw at us, it's a given that we are going to fail at something. We are going to forget. We are going to drop the ball. We are going to make some mistakes. And yes, we are going to fall short.

I am not saying to celebrate your shortcomings, but you better have your "talk with Jesus" moment and get back at it! As of today, make the promise to yourself that you will not:

- Think you have to be perfect.
- Think you have to fix everything for everybody.
- Think you have to succeed at everything.

We teach people how to treat us; honestly, it begins with us learning how to treat ourselves. Let's normalize giving ourselves the grace to thrive and be the best version of ourselves in every way. Who cares if you burned dinner, forgot to take the laundry out of the washer and put it in the dryer, or were a little late to your child's basketball game. The world is still turning, and if God lets you live another day, it's another opportunity to try and get it right. Girl, learn to give yourself some grace!

Write down some opportunities where you can extend grace to yourself. Be specific in how you will do so and sustain that habit.

_____

_____

_____

_____

_____

_____

_____

_____

Tamara M. Gordon

_____

_____

_____

_____

_____

_____

_____

_____

_____

_____

_____

_____

_____

_____

_____

_____

_____

Prayer

Loving God, here I am again, asking for your continued grace and mercy. Help me to be empathetic to all of your children by giving them the benefit of the doubt through grace. Lord, teach me especially the importance and value of giving grace to myself. Quell my tendency to want to be perfect and help me take it easy on myself in times when I fall short. Father, continue to show me an abundance of your love, grace, and mercy so that I may continue to be a light to others. In Jesus' name, Amen.

You Are What You Eat

Proverbs 23:7

For as he thinks in his heart, so is he. Eat and drink! he says to you, But his heart is not with you.

Proverbs 17:22

A joyful heart is good medicine, but a crushed spirit dries up the bones.

When I was told "eat your vegetables" as a kid, it was peas and carrots from a can and not the coveted maple glazed brussel sprouts and asparagus as we know today. Suffice it to say, I only ate them when an adult was watching, but I did recognize the small benefit when I did as told. By now, we all know there is a correlation between health benefits and diet. Empirical data strongly proves that, as humans, we are what we eat. Year after year, we promise that we will make better selections and eat healthier, but few of us stick with said promises despite knowing the benefits. Sure, junk food will give us fleeting energy, but healthy foods support health and wellness, fight against disease, and increase the durability and longevity of our human vessel. On a vanity front, proper nutrition becomes critical in our hair, skin, and nail health. For the record, I am not just referencing edible food. I am talking about the things we see, hear, practice, digest, witness, and even think on a daily basis. Just as we try to be mindful of the foods we eat, it is equally important to check our mental and spiritual diet and make the changes that will improve our well-being.

What are you feeding your spirit? Think about it. If you are always around people who live in misery and speak negativity, that is what you will eventually take on. It will certainly be your demise if you entertain a "why me?" and "I can't win" mentality. Why? Because you are what you consume. Even if you're in a good place emotionally right now, a lack of positivity can drag you down and take you out of the game. Spiritually speaking, our lives suffer when we do not get enough spiritual nutrition. This may encompass reading your Bible more or just spending the time to foster a deeper relationship with God. Whatever that looks like for you, do it. Your spirit will thank you later.

To restore or gain a positive mindset, you must first commit yourself to consuming ONLY positive thoughts. Wake up grateful each day and expect positive things to happen to you. Don't live in la-la land, but don't dwell on your problems and issues too much. Stop taking yourself too seriously. Learn to laugh and smile throughout the day. Do NOT compromise your happiness. Be intentional about how you love yourself. Set and enforce clear boundaries. And while you may not want me to include these two things, make a decent effort to eat better and exercise. The only way to break the habit of eating poorly is by cultivating a taste for nourishing and satisfying food. It takes eating "good food" to develop an appreciation for it. Beware, though! Old habits do not die quick. In other words, this will be a work in progress and not something that will happen overnight.

Your challenge for today is to change your physical and spiritual diet. Start with your mind, and the rest will follow. Whether you need to get out of the poverty mindset or the "woe is me" mentality, it all begins in the mind. God wants us to have the very best and to be the very best, and we cannot do either by consuming any and everything. So, whether you need to add snow peas to the dinner menu or change your friendship circle, do not delay. YOU ARE WHAT YOU EAT! So, choose wisely.

Write down three things you will change in your physical and spiritual diet.

_____

_____

_____

_____

_____

_____

_____

_____

Tamara M. Gordon

How will making these changes benefit you and help you achieve your goals?

_____

_____

_____

_____

_____

_____

_____

_____

_____

_____

_____

_____

_____

_____

_____

_____

_____

Prayer

Dear Father, I want to thank you just for giving me life. Lord, I need your help to be a good steward over my body, both physically and spiritually. Lord, I realize that I need your help to get on track with my spiritual and physical life. Show me the lifestyle changes I need to make and help me to make wise choices in what I place into my temple and my mind. Help me to learn to replace unhealthy things with valuable items to restore energy. Lord, please give me peace when I rest at night and help my body to fight all impurities and diseases. I declare that I will live the life you have for me. All these things I ask in your name. Amen.

When Will It Be My Turn?

Luke 12:32

Fear not little flock, for it is My Father's good pleasure to give you the kingdom.

Psalm 23:1-6

A Psalm of David. The Lord is my shepherd; I shall not want. He makes me lie down in green pastures. He leads me beside still waters. He restores my soul. He leads me in paths of righteousness for his name's sake. Even though I walk through the valley of the shadow of death, I will fear no evil, for you are with me; your rod and your staff, they comfort me. You prepare a table before me in the presence of my enemies; you anoint my head with oil; my cup overflows.

Tamara M. Gordon

When am I going to get the new car that I want?
OMG! When did I hit age 40?
When will I have the financial freedom to do what I want?
Why am I the only one of my friends not engaged to be married?
Why am I not living the life I feel I deserve?
When am I going to take my dream vacation?
Why don't I have my own family?

A close girlfriend and I find ourselves having some long, deep discussions every holiday season. As realists and Christians (yes, you can be both), we talk about how, in our 20s and early 30s, it was extremely important to our public image to do things the "right" way. We admitted that we hated feeling that way and recognized the pressure we put on ourselves during our earlier years. In a small way, there was a bit of relief knowing that we were not alone in the way we felt. With Black women especially, there seems to be a much larger spotlight on our upbringing and whether we are successful in life. Then you have to deal with the pressures of your social life or lack thereof. At every holiday dinner party with family, it seems commonplace for someone to broach the topic of your dating status and plans for the future. Honestly, it becomes annoying. Albeit unintentional, placing invisible checkboxes for young women to feel like they have to check off pushes them to measure themselves against their peers. This is often when self-doubt comes into play.

Have you ever found yourself in a place where you feel as if love seemed to have lost your name? Has the desires of your heart failed to knock on your door? Truth is, all of us are waiting for something and hope our turn is coming. It could be that you are waiting on a career promotion or a chance to launch a new business opportunity. Or maybe you are waiting to find that forever love or the chance to own the home of your dreams. At the end of the day, your desires versus the wait can make it feel brutal and like these things will never be granted, but maybe you're not as ready as you think you are. My comment may have left you speechless, but seriously, you may be praying for something you are not prepared for if you were to get it right now. Have you ever considered that? One thing for sure is that God knows everything before it happens, and He desires to give us our heart's desires, but only when the time is right. I know it is aggravating and can seem unfair, especially when those around you are getting everything they want. But this delay isn't a denial. Your turn is coming!

When you become impatient and even bitter with God, think of Abraham, who waited until he was one hundred years old to get an heir. God blessed Abraham and Sarah with Isaac according to His faith. Genesis 15:4-5 reads: *And behold, the word of the LORD came to him, saying, "This one shall not be your heir, but one who will come from your own body shall be your heir." 5Then He brought him outside and said, "Look now toward heaven, and count the stars if you are able to number them." And He said to him, "So shall your descendants be."*

Don't be distracted by discontentment in waiting. Remind yourself that what you're waiting for is worth it and that God will always keep His promises to you. Celebrate those around you who are having their turn. Make all the progress you need right where you are in the interim. Lastly, when you feel the urge to want to throw in the towel, don't do it! Stay the course because your turn just might be next! It is no secret what God can do. What He's done for others, He'll do for you.

Tamara M. Gordon

How patient are you when it comes to waiting for what you want?

_____

_____

_____

_____

_____

_____

_____

_____

_____

_____

_____

_____

_____

_____

_____

_____

_____

What are you doing in this season of waiting to ensure you are ready when your turn comes?

_____

_____

_____

_____

_____

_____

_____

_____

_____

_____

_____

_____

_____

_____

_____

_____

Tamara M. Gordon

Prayer

Dear Lord, help me to learn the value of waiting on you. Remind me that all good things come from you and that you will not withhold any good from me. Remove the urge to compare my life with those around me and help me to understand that only your will be done. Grant me the peace of knowing you are always working it out. When I am anxious about life, help me recall Psalm 130:5: "I will wait for the LORD, my soul waits, and in his word I hope." Help me to be patient as I wait as long as it takes. In Jesus' name, Amen.

Tired of Taking These L's

Psalm 34:18

The Lord is near to the brokenhearted and saves the crushed in spirit.

Psalm 73:26

My flesh and my heart faileth: but God is the strength of my heart, and my portion forever.

2 Corinthians 2:14

Now thanks be unto God, which always causeth us to triumph in Christ.

One of my favorite tracks by gospel artist Jekalyn Carr is "You Will Win". Every morning, I listen to this to help place me in a mindset of conquering anything standing in my way. The lyrics touch me in a unique way, and I am sure it will do the same for you.

Tamara M. Gordon

The enemy came up against your home
The enemy came up against your children
The enemy came up against your Name
The enemy came up against your character

You will win, win
You will win, win

The enemy came up against your health
The enemy came up against your finance
The enemy came up against your vision
The enemy came up against your business

No matter how much we try to do the right thing, part of life is understanding that sometimes terrible things happen to good people. This notion is true and is not predicated on the good you've done, the service you've rendered, or the life you've lived. The interesting thing about this is that we grow up being taught and believing that if we do good, good will be returned to us in the same measure. But it is not that simple.

By now, I am sure you have experienced discouragement, disagreement, disappointment, and rejection—and I know it can be heavy. Some days, it may even seem like you can't win for losing. Despite the constant obstacles that life throws at you, I promise you that God wants you to win. You read that right. It doesn't matter how bleak things look now; God has the final say and is always in control. Winning with God isn't just spiritual either. He wants you to win in your finances, profession, relationships, and other areas of your life. I would go so far as to say that if you're not at least in the process of thinking like a winner, you're not fulfilling God's whole purpose for your life. Now, I know that is a mouthful, but there is no better time than the present to help you start thinking, believing, and moving like a winner.

God makes it plain in the book of Genesis that we are made in His image, and that is something we should stand on. I think we all can agree that God is a winner, and therefore, we are, too. Don't buy into this mentality that being a Christian means living lowly, struggling, and being in need. That is false. All of us can watch a champion, but how many of us want to do the work to become one? Philippians is a book about winning written by a winner— the apostle Paul. Paul took all kinds of L's, left and right, but never allowed them to determine his faith or future.

Life can be something else and come at you fast. The enemy will attack you through your family, finances, and health. When that doesn't work, he will use your relationships or job. Just know that as we go through stuff, there is victory on the other side. Winning is not about having it all together right now. It is about knowing we'll be in the best position when it is all said and done. When you are feeling down on yourself and nothing is going your way, read Philippians 3:13-14 where Paul says, "Brethren, I count not myself to have apprehended: but this one thing I do, forgetting those things which are behind, and reaching forth unto those things which are before. I press toward the mark for the prize of the high calling of God in Christ Jesus." This passage is at the heart of winning. So, embrace it and change your tune from "woe is me" to "all I do is win, win, win no matter what." Remember, anybody can fight, but will you win?

Tamara M. Gordon

What steps will you take to change your mindset to that of a winner?

_____

_____

_____

_____

_____

_____

_____

_____

_____

_____

_____

_____

_____

_____

_____

_____

_____

Have you ever experienced a situation where it looked like you lost, but in hindsight, you won?

_____

_____

_____

_____

_____

_____

_____

_____

_____

_____

_____

_____

_____

_____

Tamara M. Gordon

Prayer

Father God, thank you for showing me that greater is in me than he that is in the world. Father, thank you for holding up a standard against my enemies. I praise you for keeping me grounded in my losing seasons and humble in my winning seasons. Lord, help me take my hands off every battle I am currently facing and will face because I know the battle is not mine but yours. Remind me to allow you to defend my name and honor amongst man so that you can get all the praise and glory in our triumph. Amen.

Quitting Is No Longer an Option

Hebrews 12:1-2

Let us run with perseverance the race marked out for us, fixing our eyes on Jesus, the pioneer and perfecter of faith.

2 CHRONICLES 20:12

O our God, wilt thou do not judge them? for we have no might against this great company that cometh against us; neither know we what to do

*Y*ou either quit or keep going. Both hurt, so don't quit! Let me keep it 100 with you; sometimes, I wish I could just quit! Like walk away, throw in the towel, and be done with it, but I just cannot. When I think about it now, there are some things I quit too soon and others I carried too long. As a child, my dad made us learn how to play an instrument. I am not sure if I chose or he did, but I took piano lessons. At first, I was excited about learning to play. However, my interest dwindled as I got older and began to like boys and sports. I was good, too! Against my young judgment, I quit and regret that decision even today. If you are a woman, you have your own stories regarding your struggles. It could be financial ruin, a troubled family member, job loss, relational issues, or mental, emotional, or physical illnesses. Whatever the trouble or problem, we struggle with the thought of quitting.

There will be times when you're doing everything you know to do and still don't see any progress. The Israelites walked around Jericho for six days straight, and nothing happened as far as they could see. I'm certain many of them wanted to tap out, and I'm sure somebody somewhere may have taken a break or two. But Joshua held to what God said when he told him seven times. After the seventh time, the walls of Jericho did come down. Whatever you have in your life as your wall can also come down. Just because you don't see God working does not mean He isn't. Sure, we gave up too early before and missed a few blessings as a result. This time, we are holding the line and completing the task. Quitting is no longer an option.

We recognize that the promises of God are yes and amen (2 Corinthians 1:20). Suppose the Israelites had quit. What if they bounced the second time around? Like many of us, they would have missed the blessing of the wall coming down. Whew! Read that line again. We would have missed out. We all have a petition with the Lord, and I cannot tell you when the victory is coming. But I do know tomorrow could be your final lap, and I would hate for you to miss out. Stay hydrated and stay in the race, y'all, because quitting is not an option. It's our winning season!

Have you learned a lesson from quitting something in the past? If so, how did it affect you?

_____

_____

_____

_____

_____

_____

_____

_____

_____

_____

_____

_____

_____

_____

_____

_____

Tamara M. Gordon

Prayer

Dear Lord, I look to you to settle my mind when I want to give up. You encourage my heart even in the most challenging times, and I thank you. Thank you for your examples of victory. Help me to remain faithful and trusting of you. Please give me the strength to persevere, even when I'm tempted to quit. In Jesus' name, Amen.

Be Humble, Sit Down!

John 5:30
I can do nothing on my own. As I hear, I judge, and my judgment is just because I seek not my own will but the will of him who sent me.

1 Peter 5:5
Likewise, you who are younger, be subject to the elders. Clothe yourselves, all of you, with humility toward one another, for "God opposes the proud but gives grace to the humble."

There is nothing wrong with confidence or assuredness. Nothing. In fact, both are necessary to have a productive and satisfying life. However, when one's confidence turns into them thinking no one can tell them NOTHING, it is time for them to check their ego. The ego is a person's sense of self-importance, and while it serves some value, it can also cause our spiritual demise. If we are serious about our walks with God, we have to understand that our need to be praised and validated must be at bay. Throughout the Bible, an inflated sense of self is shown to be destructive, which is how the devil got his first role as Lucifer. His ego led him to believe he was on the same level as God. Welp, we all know that ended in his banishment, and he has been tripping ever since.

The opposite of ego is humility. 1 Peter 5:5 epitomizes why we are to be humble: *All of you, clothe yourselves with humility toward one another, because God opposes the proud but gives grace to the humble.* Humility is one of the most powerful and essential attributes of maturity and growth. The humblest story in the Bible is Jesus washing the feet of His disciples, including Judas, who He knows will betray Him. Many of us cannot humble ourselves enough to speak to someone who has done us wrong, much less wash the dirtiest part of their body. Jesus told them the lesson that leaders are called to be servants. He then tells them that to be a leader, one must first be a servant. Jesus promises they will be blessed if they do the same. I know personally that humble people can receive a bad rap. Humility is often confused with being too passive or insecure, but this couldn't be further from the truth. Being humble is the real flex. We are confident and competent in ourselves so much that, as a result, we seek to help others. Being humble should never be confused with what you cannot do; it is a choice to do what you should do without the impetus to brag.

Humility begins with accepting who we are and understanding that it is not always about us. Yes, I know that in the world we live in now, it is counter-cultural to seek out the humble and meek. Society places a lot of weight on the people making the rules and those who are loud, flashy, and popular. But, believe me, as you age and grow, the value of humility within and with our circle will be unmatched. After all, there is a time and place for everything, even to...Be Humble and Sit Down!

How can you show more gratitude and become humbler?

_____

_____

_____

_____

_____

_____

_____

_____

_____

_____

_____

_____

_____

_____

_____

Tamara M. Gordon

How will you demonstrate humility in your ups and downs in life?

_____

_____

_____

_____

_____

_____

_____

_____

_____

_____

_____

_____

_____

_____

_____

_____

Prayer

Merciful Father, on this day, I am asking for your help to live humbly. Help me not think more highly of myself than I ought but to delight in regarding others as more important. Help me to value all of your children and be accountable to you. Lord, keep me focused on the big picture so that I may obey your commandment to love one another to build a better kingdom. In Jesus' name, Amen.

The Giant Is Your Help

Ephesians 6:12

For we do not wrestle against flesh and blood, but against the rulers, against the authorities, against the cosmic powers over this present darkness, against the spiritual forces of evil in the heavenly places.

Romans 8:31

What then shall we say to these things? If God is for us, who can be against us. We all face distinct kinds of giants in our lives. The question isn't whether they'll show up; it's whether we'll have the courage and faith to defeat them. I've been in battle with giants at different stages in my life and I would be a liar if I told you I was not afraid. See, the giants that we see are at least visible, but try defeating an unseen giant that comes in the form of serious health issues. Not easy to do! Some of you may find yourself in a battle with a financial giant or a spiritual giant; the outcome is the same and you will defeat it.

Tamara M. Gordon

*T*he story of David defeating Goliath is still a fascinating parable in the Bible. It shows how young David is first willing to step forward and face a physically aggressive and skilled enemy all by himself. By earthly standards, David was woefully unprepared, or as we say, "not ready," to engage Goliath. However, in the biblical sense, David had all the traits anybody would want in a future king: bravery, smarts, boldness, and a willingness to lead. Picture this: Goliath, over nine feet tall and covered in more than 125 pounds of armor, was in a fight with young little David. Not what the streets call a "fair one," except the Lord was on David's side.

David's confidence in the Lord was well-placed, and ours should be, also. For each of us born, God has continuously shown us His unmerited favor and brand-new mercies daily. There is no reason to believe He will stop now. We don't have to be fearful when we receive bad news or go through an unpredictable storm. Fear is no match for God, who is on our side. Before every promotion or major move of the Lord, there will be a fight, storm, or challenge of some kind. Even in this parable, David needed Goliath. Goliath was not there to take him out. Instead, he was there to show that David was more than a shepherd boy. In today's terms, Goliath put David "on!" The king would have never considered David for king if he had not defeated what he thought would kill him.

When facing our fears, we will recall the qualities of this young shepherd and dare to be David. From the story of David and Goliath, we can learn that God is capable of defeating any of the giants in our lives—fear, depression, relationship problems, financial issues, and everything else—if we let Him. For as long as we live, we will face a giant of some kind, but we must remember the giant is there to help us get to the next level. Get your slingshot and plan your victory party because we already know how this one will end!

What are you up against right now in your life?

_____

_____

_____

_____

_____

_____

_____

_____

_____

_____

_____

_____

_____

_____

Tamara M. Gordon

What skills do you personally have that can overcome your giant?

_____

_____

_____

_____

_____

_____

_____

_____

_____

_____

_____

_____

_____

_____

_____

_____

Prayer

Heavenly Father, you know me better than I know myself, and you see the giants I'm facing even before I see them. Thank you for being more than enough to conquer them all on my behalf. Thank you for sending your spirit as a comfort in the midst of my storms and battles. Father, instill in me the courage to fight any giant up against me and to be prepared for battle with you as my help. As I load my slingshot and point it towards the target, I trust you. In Jesus' name, Amen.

In Spite of Me

Romans 5:8

But God demonstrates his own love for us in this: While we were still sinners, Christ died for us. His encouraging message to you is that God loves you so much, even though you are messed up, he gave that which was the most valuable to him, so you could know him.

Romans 8:39

Nothing can separate us from the love of God which is in Christ Jesus

Tamara M. Gordon

Some days are better than others
I can be up, then I'm down
But beyond my mistakes
I'm found in Your grace
And this one thing will never change

You still love me in spite of me
You still chose me
How can it be?
Every scar, every flaw, You see it all
You see it all. You still love me, love me
In spite of me

~ Tasha Cobbs Leonard

*H*ave you ever wondered if God still loved you after you sinned? Did you feel He would abandon you because you repeatedly committed the same sin? Have you wondered if He is still on your team, especially since He knows all your thoughts? Whew! I don't know about you, but just thinking about my past makes me thankful for God's enduring love. So, in regards to the question of whether God loves you even when you knowingly sin, the simple answer is YES!

God has loved me through my mistakes, bad ideas, poor decisions, failures, and other mess! Unlike man, He loves us in spite of ourselves. Therefore, we should feel no shame in messing up because as long as we live, we will all fall short at some time or another. So, forgive yourself for that opportunity you fumbled or the relationship you tip-toed on. Stop beating yourself up over that deal you made that went bad or the time you acted outside of your character. With God, we can always start over because His love is unconditional and everlasting. I am still amazed that God knows my name; He loved me through it all. We will never be able to understand God's unwavering love in our finite minds. Despite us repeatedly messing up, His love is still right there. My friends, you don't even have the ability to make God not love you—now that's deep!

Understand this: God's love for you did not begin with your honorable deeds or behavior, and it won't end when you go astray. He is not in love with you because of your occupation, the degrees you hold, or your titles. God is not pressed or impressed with any of that. His love is based on the fact that you are His child. That's it. Nothing else. You can't make God love you more, and you can't make him love you less. He loves you just as much on your bad days as on your good ones. God does not love any of us more than the next one; He loves all His children the same. Yes, this includes those who are right, wrong, or walking the line of the in-between.

Does God love me? The greatest evidence of God's love is Jesus' crucifixion. Add to that, there is no love like the love of God. As much as I love my family, friends, church members, and peers, I have failed them in some way or another. But in Jeremiah 31:3, God says, "I have loved you with an everlasting love. With unfailing love, I have drawn you to myself." In simpler terms, there is no love measurable to that of God.

Jesus loves me! This I know,
For the Bible tells me so;
Little ones to Him belong;
They are weak, but He is strong.

Tamara M. Gordon

Refrain:
Yes, Jesus loves me!
Yes, Jesus loves me!
Yes, Jesus loves me!
The Bible tells me so. ~ Anna B. Warner

How does it make you feel to realize that God loves you despite your failures?

_____

_____

_____

_____

_____

_____

_____

_____

_____

_____

_____

_____

_____

How will you share the message of God's love with those who believe they have disappointed Him?

_____

_____

_____

_____

_____

_____

_____

_____

_____

_____

_____

_____

_____

_____

_____

_____

Prayer

Heavenly Father, thank you for letting me experience true unconditional love. In a world where people base their love on earthly things, I am grateful for knowing I am one of your own. Lord, I bless you for filling the void of love from humankind and holding me close when I thought loneliness would consume me. Thank you for giving me loving family and friends that do their best to show up in love. Help me to remember that you love me in spite of me, even when I fall short. Thank you, Lord Jesus, for loving me so much that nothing in my past, present, or future can separate me from you. In Jesus' name, Amen.

What's The Plan, God?

John 15.16

You did not choose me, but I chose you and appointed you that you should go and bear fruit and that your fruit should abide, so that whatever you ask the Father in my name, he may give it to you.

1 Peter 2:9

But you are a chosen race, a royal priesthood, a consecrated nation, a [special] people for God's own possession, so that you may proclaim the excellencies [the wonderful deeds and virtues and perfections] of Him who called you out of darkness into His marvelous light.

We all have experienced the nervousness and feeling of waiting to be chosen by somebody. Whether it was to be on a team in elementary based on our athleticism or for a promotion based on work ethic, we have been in situations where there was a chance we could be disappointed. Your disappointment may have come during your quest to join a sorority or musical team. Or the dreaded desire to be chosen by a love interest or long-time crush, only to find out you are not their type. Extremely disappointing, right? While the situations may vary, we all have firsthand accounts of how it made us feel. Truth is, we will be chosen more times than not in most cases.

God has been choosing people since the earth's foundation, beginning with the birth of His son. He chose Mary; she did not choose Him. In fact, she was shocked when she understood she did not have a choice in the matter, even as a virgin. Imagine today, saying you are a virgin, yet you get pregnant and then deliver a baby. This would be the *tea of all tea* now, but I am sure it was something to gossip about even back then. Being chosen will often bring conflict and sometimes even criticism. It is not always butterflies, glitter, and rainbows to be in that coveted spot. Think about it. To carry the savior in your womb would be incredible, but the same mother had to witness the horrible death of the son she delivered. From the outside looking in, people always want the spot of the chosen one. It seems like the place to be because they witness the spotlight but not the sadness. They see the lights but not the lies. They see perceived power but never the pain. Yeah, that's all a part of being chosen. Like Mary and her feelings of trepidation, the same is true today because people are the same. People are often jealous of what they don't know or can't have. To make matters worse, they often miss their own chosen path because they are too busy worrying about the path of others.

I do not care how someone else's life may look. Stop wishing you had someone else's life. I'm here to tell you that you don't want that smoke because you are not equipped to handle it like them. God chose them to do something, and He has chosen you to do something else! You cannot walk in their destiny, nor can they walk in yours.

For a long while, I spent a lot of time trying to stifle my gifts, but I was never quite successful. Not wanting to be labeled too ambitious or offend someone who may have been insecure about something, I tried to stay quiet or hide in the shadows. It almost killed me to suppress myself, and God kept me so uncomfortable in that place. The Bible says, *You were chosen according to the purpose of God the Father and were made a holy people by his Spirit. (1 Peter 1:2)* The benefit of understanding that you have been chosen is that you don't have to long for the approval or acceptance of anyone else. No matter how daunting the task or assignment in your life, God is with you, and you will come out on top.

We usually want to know God's plan for our life when it comes to relationships, big decisions, and other practical matters. But the Lord's priority will always be our spiritual wellness. When we get that part right, He will direct us in every other aspect of our lives. Today is the perfect day to start walking in the plan with your name on it. Once you do, you will see God move in your life to defend that plan, promote that plan, and bless that plan.

Where do you want God to take you in life?

_____

_____

_____

_____

_____

Tamara M. Gordon

Write down your plan to pray for the next 3, 5, and 10 years of your life.

_____

_____

_____

_____

_____

_____

_____

_____

_____

_____

_____

_____

_____

_____

_____

_____

Tamara M. Gordon

Prayer

Dear Heavenly Father, thank you for mapping out the plan and success for my life. Help me to hear your calling and accept it. Help me to stay focused on your plan so that I may have favor in every way. God, I thank you for choosing me and helping me make it to the finish line. Amen.

Flow, Not Forced

Zechariah 4:6

"Not by might, nor by power, but by My Spirit says the Lord Almighty."

Philippians 1:6

"For I am confident of this very thing, that He who began a good work in you will perfect it until the day of Christ Jesus."

As a little girl, my mother would always take me to buy new school shoes. I would get excited because she would allow me to pick out any shoe I liked as long as it was age-appropriate and a "good" shoe. When we got to the mall, I would look around, pick out a few favorites, and ask the sales associate for my size. I cannot recall what size I needed in middle school, but I distinctly remember wanting the coveted navy blue Sabego loafers one year. The sales associate brought out all the selections, and of course, the pair I liked the most was too small. But I didn't let it on to my mother, even though I was told to try on both shoes and walk around the store to make sure they felt good on my feet. Let's just say I could have earned an Emmy. My mother made the purchase with minimum debate, and we left.

A few weeks later, when school started, I squeezed my feet into those shoes, knowing full well they were too small. I was able to handle the snug fit for a few hours, but by the end of the day, there was no denying that forcing my feet into a too-small shoe was not the best thing to do. When my mother asked how my day was at school, I told her and snuck in the fact that the shoes I had begged her for were uncomfortable. Well, I'm sure you can guess what followed, but eventually, I got shoes in my correct size.

I was young and impressionable then, allowing my desire to have the popular shoe to outweigh my common sense. The idea of forcing things to "fit" is a lifetime concept we often make the mistake of doing. In life, we will encounter people who we want to get to know better or have a romantic relationship with so much that we find ourselves trying to force it. When you gain anything due to force, you will always second-guess the purpose or authenticity as related to you. We've all had that feeling or heard that little voice telling us not to do something, and we ignore it because we want something so much in that moment. In doing so, I am sure many, like myself, have suffered the consequences of immediate satisfaction.

If you know you don't want the job, don't force it. If a love interest is unsure if they want to be with you or is not reciprocal, don't force it. If you believe there is someone that you could become besties with, but they are not in alignment, don't force it. If you want the car or house but know the note is out of your budget and the interest is too high, don't force it. God has a way of looking out for us—or at least tries—when he puts us in situations to recognize a flow versus a force. We mess up whenever we ignore His signs and listen to our flesh instead or take what is in front of us. As we grow in God, we should always consider how His words and nudges guided people in the biblical days and still do if we are humble enough to hear them and obedient enough to follow through. As we are met with different scenarios, we may allow ourselves only to see and hear what we want to be true, but when we ask for discernment and truly seek God for guidance, His way will reveal itself without confusion or opposition. I don't want to scare you, but interestingly enough, you will make some bad calls along the way. That is all part of the process. My mother would always quote my grandmother, saying, "It don't have to be this hard if you would have listened to me the first time." Now, as an adult, I know this to be true and say the same thing to my son.

So, while this excerpt started with a story about a shoe for school, it is not about that at all. The bottom line is that God wants to take our lives from forced to flow. He does not call for us to be in any situation with anybody where we have to force anything. In fact, He is just that good that if it is from Him, He will line everything up in our favor. So, yes, there will be assemblies you want to be a part of and people you want to get to know. There may be a job you want or an opportunity you want to tackle. All of that is perfectly okay if God is in it. I am not telling you not to put your best foot forward, endure a process, or pursue something. I am simply telling you not to force it.

Think of it this way: God controls everything in this world and doesn't even force us to do anything. He gives us free will, and we make our choices. The Bible is full of lessons that teach the importance of free will and the consequences of it. We will no longer want something so desperately that we force things to happen in order to try to get the results we want. From this day forward, we will wait for God's direction and let it flow.

Name a situation where you knew it was not for you, but you forced it to happen.

_____

_____

_____

_____

_____

_____

_____

_____

_____

_____

_____

_____

_____

_____

How did it end, and what did you learn from it?

_____

_____

_____

_____

_____

_____

_____

_____

_____

_____

_____

_____

_____

_____

_____

_____

_____

_____

Prayer

Loving Father, I want to give control over my life and yield it into your hands. Please teach me how to let go so I am not impulsive in my decisions that will affect myself and others. Lord, please speak to me so that I may hear and understand what you want me to do. Give me good signs, good discernment, and better judgment as I grow stronger in you. Lord, help me to live in the flow instead of the force. Amen.

I Can't Go Back

Psalm 51:10

Create in me a clean heart, O God, and renew a steadfast spirit within me."

Romans 12:2

Do not be conformed to this world, but be transformed by the renewal of your mind, that by testing you may discern what is the will of God, what is good, acceptable, and perfect.

They are stuck in their ways. That's just how they are. We've all heard this said before, and if we are honest with ourselves, we have used this statement to excuse people's often rude and unacceptable behavior. It is not okay because we all know we are indeed in control (or should be) of our behavior, especially as adults. Truth be told, change is one of the hardest things to do. Think about it. Everybody has something they could stand to change, and they would if it was easy and didn't require sacrifices: weight, unhealthy habits, attitude, and everything in between. Change is hard, even with the best intentions, and the struggle is real. That's because when it comes to lasting change, God has to be a part of it for it to stick.

The Apostle Paul is one of the best-known figures in the Bible. Paul had two names. His Jewish name was Saul, and his Roman name was Paul. The letters he wrote thousands of years ago are still vital for us today. They give us life and understanding, instruction and hope. Paul's transformation is a shining example for each of us who are trying day by day to be a better person and make a change.

Saul was a zealous Jew born in the city of Tarsus but who grew up in Jerusalem. He studied under the best Jewish teachers, including the well-respected teacher Gamaliel (Acts 22:3). The first time Saul is mentioned in the New Testament is in Acts 7:58 and 8:1. Saul stood in approval of the stoning of Stephen and went so far as to look after the clothes of those who threw the stones. Saul believed in Jesus but did not follow Him. Instead, he violently attempted to wipe out the followers of Jesus, even all the way to Damascus. Understanding this simple description of Saul is necessary to see the drastic change that would take place in his life. What happened on the road to Damascus was nothing shy of a miracle of God.

Saul asked to carry letters to the city of Damascus because he thought he could convince the people there to hate the followers of Christ. As he and his companions walked along the road to Damascus, something unexpected happened. A bright light shone down, and everyone stopped. The light blinded Saul. The group saw the light and could hear something, but only Paul could hear a voice that said, "Saul, Saul, why are you persecuting me?" Meanwhile, in another part of the city, there was a man called Ananias who followed

Jesus. In a vision, Jesus told him to meet Saul. Ananias thought Jesus was tripping, as Saul was persecuting people like him. However, because of his conviction, he obeyed Jesus' command. He went to Straight Street and found Saul. He touched Saul and advised him that Jesus had sent him. In that time, Saul (now Paul) was able to see and went on to tell everyone in Damascus about his change. Many people began to believe in Jesus when they heard Saul preach.

Much like Saul, not everyone will be supportive when we make changes in our lives for the better. You may change your attitude, outlook, prior decision, or even how you feel about someone, and chances are there will be someone around you who is not happy about it.

This is nothing new. Even in the days of Saul, some people were furious. They got so caught up in their feelings that they made plans to kill him. Jesus changed Saul from the person he was and began using him to preach. After the life he led, the people he murdered, and even the chaos he fostered, Saul recognized that where he was going was far better than where he had come from. We all have something or somebody in our past that we think of going back to. On the right day and at the right time, it will play in our minds like the best thing since sliced bread. But, in our honesty, we know that would not be wise. There will be some days where you want to go back and, dare I say, may actually go back, but understand that is not where you belong. As with Saul, when God changes something in us for the better, we have to be strong enough during our journey to look back but not go there.

Tamara M. Gordon

Name a trait you know is hindering you from being your best self.

_____

_____

_____

_____

_____

_____

_____

_____

_____

_____

_____

_____

_____

_____

_____

_____

_____

Decide a few intentional things you will do to minimize the negativity of those traits.

Tamara M. Gordon

What positive thing can you use to replace something negative in your life?

_____

_____

_____

_____

_____

_____

_____

_____

_____

_____

_____

_____

_____

_____

_____

_____

Prayer

It's me, oh Lord, standing in the need of prayer. Lord, I ask you to be my constant guide and continue walking by my side. I know there are some things that need to be ironed out in my life, and I recognize that I cannot do it on my own. I have some struggles that I am placing in your hands to help me move from myself and into your will for my life. Lord, when I am tempted to give up or even go back, I trust that you will lead me your way and keep me on this journey. I won't go back! Amen.

Use What You Got!

Colossians 1:16

For in him all things were created: things in heaven and on earth, visible and invisible, whether thrones, powers, rulers, or authorities; all things have been created through him and for him.

Mark 6:41–44

And when he had taken the five loaves and the two fishes, he looked up to heaven, and blessed, and broke the loaves, and gave them to his disciples to set before them; and the two fishes divided he among them all. And they all eat and were filled. And they took up twelve baskets full of the fragments, and of the fishes. And they that did eat of the loaves were about five thousand men.

Most of us are familiar with one of the parables in the Bible where there was not enough food for a large hungry crowd, and Jesus performed the miracle with little fish and bread. Whether you know the story of the disciples' packed lunch being the starting point of the miracle or the small boy giving his single serving to Jesus, the point remains the same. Jesus was known for taking what was already there and multiplying it for thousands. These stories demonstrate that Jesus makes abundance for his people. While Jesus was healing the sick and feeding the poor, there were two groups of people with things to say. A hungry mass of people were followers of Jesus who wanted an opportunity to gain experience from Him and possibly be blessed. The others were the Pharisees who kept trying Jesus by asking him to show them signs from heaven. Without a doubt, Jesus declined their audacity. Here, we see the discernment of Jesus as he manages the motives of these two groups appropriately and accordingly. He rewarded the hungry followers with food because of their faith, and the Pharisees were met with nothing.

We are always tempted to believe we can do more if we have more. This thought process threatens our happiness, success, and motivation. Thinking you cannot do remarkable things until you are in a "better" position is just a distraction. When you are distracted, it is impossible to complete any decent work in you. Sure, it may be easier if you had more, but God is clear in the Bible that He has always shown up and given a surplus with less. If you find yourself in a season of waiting on "more" to get started or even to finish, meditate on the biblical recording of the feeding of the multitudes. I don't care if you need more resources, money, time, support, and faith. God is the keeper of all you need to get it done now.

The book of Genesis tells us that God created the earth out of absolutely nothing. Surely, if God can create an entire world from scratch, He can provide all that we need to conquer it. Seriously, think about it! If God can create this whole landscape and place man on it, what more can He do in our lives? With God, you can and will do it. He is our safety net and our guarantee to prosper. It does not matter if the timing doesn't seem right. It does not matter if your finances are not looking right. It will not even matter if your faith is not right. God has the master plan, and He has proven Himself over and over again. He is the only one who takes nothing and makes much. So, until He blesses you with more, USE WHAT YOU GOT!

How do you cope with doubt? What do you tell yourself when you have a big goal to achieve but your confidence is low?

_____

_____

_____

_____

_____

_____

_____

_____

_____

_____

Tamara M. Gordon

What do you have now that can be used to get you to where you want to be?

_____

_____

_____

_____

_____

_____

_____

_____

_____

_____

_____

_____

_____

_____

_____

_____

_____

Prayer

Lord, I want to thank you for bringing me to the place I am right now. Lord, although I may be weary, afraid, and tired, I am counting on you like you have instructed me to do. I know you have assigned me my portion and my cup. You have made my lot secure, and for that, I thank you. Lord, I know you have gone before me and have already made a way out of no way and prepared my cup for overflow. I will trust and praise you, Lord, for all the blessings you are preparing me for because I know they are on the way. You have made known to me the path of life. You will fill me with joy in your presence, with eternal pleasures at your right hand (Psalm 16:5-11). In Jesus' name, Amen.

Purpose In Your Pain

Psalm 119:71

My suffering was good for me, for it taught me to pay attention to your decrees.

Romans 5:3–4

Not only that, but we rejoice in our sufferings, knowing that suffering produces endurance, 4 and endurance produces character, and character produces hope…

I am reminded of an old-time favorite by gospel great Kirk Franklin that says:

I've gone through the fire. And I've been through the flood.
I've been broken into pieces. Seen lightning flashing from above.
But through it all, I remember that He loves me and He cares.
And He'll never put more on me than I can bear.

Tamara M. Gordon

If you have ever been in extreme physical pain, you will understand that I sang these lyrics in my head line by line, stanza after stanza, throughout many surgeries. After mustering up the courage to have back surgery in 2012, I can only recall two things: the debilitating pain that would never let up and the recovery staff waking me up from surgery. At first thought, I felt like a miracle had occurred, but that was short-lived once the anesthesia wore off. After dozing in and out of consciousness, I woke up in tears from the new pain going through my body. I couldn't move and didn't have the strength to cry out for help. Even worse, I couldn't remember how to press the button that would distribute the medication. I was a mess.

After the first day, physical and occupational therapy were added to my regimen. The first time I tried to get up, the pain was so intense that I instantly fell back on the pillow. At the time, I was super aggravated by the one therapist adamant that I make another attempt to sit up. While rolling my eyes at her, I flinched and scowled until I was sitting up. As if that wasn't enough, she then asked me to stand up. I remember thinking, *She must be a nut.* After walking no more than five feet, I told her that I could not do much more because the pain was too great. Clearly, she already knew this because she responded, "You just underwent six hours of back surgery. Of course, you will feel pain."

We all are either suffering ourselves or know someone who is. The suffering may show up as cancer, death, illness, heartache, betrayal, loss, injustice, and many other ways, but know that even in pain, God allows a way to Him. During our pain and suffering, we can find small satisfaction in the hope that God will eventually make it alright. If that isn't enough, the visual of the empty tomb is our biblical proof that suffering does not start or end with us. It is during pain that God shows us who we are and the people around us. Pain brings out the reality in all of us. When I was struggling with pain, I would ask God, "Why is this happening to me?" Have you ever wondered about the point of your pain or suffering? Although I believed things would eventually get better, I did not see a glimmer of light at the end of the tunnel I was in then. Job 1:1 tells us, "There was a man in the land of Uz whose name was Job; and that man was perfect and upright, and one that feared God, and eschewed evil."

Job was not considered churchy, but he was the most affluent man in the East with abundant possessions. Joe had a happy, large family that consisted of a wife, seven sons, and three daughters. He owned several lots of land and cattle. In short, he had everything a man would want. (Job 1:2-3) But even in all his stuff, Job's greatest asset was his faith. Job's ability to believe was so on point that both God and Satan took notice. Long story short, Job endured an intense season of suffering that attacked him physically, emotionally, and even spiritually, but he kept his faith. All this occurred as a test allowed by God to show Job what He was made of and to show Satan that Job had unshakeable faith.

There was a point to Job's pain. Job learned lessons through his suffering that he couldn't have learned any other way. He learned patience. He learned long suffering. He learned humbleness. He learned to depend on God fully. He learned prayer like never before, and Job came out of his season of suffering with a new outlook. In fact, he said, "I had heard about you before, but now I have seen you with my own eyes." (Job 42:5) The way you need and see God is a whole different level when you are in pain. You begin to call on God in a way that only He can answer and begin to comfort you.

Are you physically, emotionally, or spiritually hurt? Is there a void of pain you feel from others or even yourself? Do you have a broken heart? Are you like me and, over the years, have developed a high threshold for the pain? Or are you temporarily numbing your pain with whatever (or whomever) will give you temporary relief? Either way, God knows all about our pain and suffering, and if we hold onto our faith and allow Him, He will show us the purpose in our pain.

Think of a painful event you endured. How did you get to the other side? How would you encourage others in a time of pain?

_____

_____

_____

_____

_____

_____

_____

_____

_____

Tamara M. Gordon

Prayer

Dear God, thank you that your kindness, sometimes even pain, is good. God, teach us to maintain the faith of Job when we are suffering and in pain. Lord, I confess that when I experience pain, my first instinct is to run toward whatever will give me quick relief despite knowing it will not sustain me. God, please show me the purpose in my pain. Open my eyes and heart so that I may understand you love me with an unmatched love and only want the best for me. Please forgive me for turning to things or people in my weakness and help me turn to you. In Jesus' name, Amen.

Turn The Page

Joshua 1:1-3

Now after the death of Moses the servant of the Lord it came to pass, that the Lord spake unto Joshua the son of Nun, Moses' minister, saying, Moses my servant is dead; now therefore arise, go over this Jordan, thou, and all this people, unto the land which I do give to them, even to the children of Israel. Every place that the sole of your foot shall tread upon, that have I given unto you, as I said unto Moses.

Isaiah 43:18-19

Remember not the former things, nor consider the things of old. Behold, I am doing a new thing; now it springs forth, do you not perceive it? I will make a way in the wilderness and rivers in the desert.

Tamara M. Gordon

*S*ometimes, the hardest thing to do is to accept what is and move on. Many of us never actually move on, which is a direct hit on destiny. I remember when I went away to college eight hours away from home. I was adamant about keeping all of my memories in my bedroom. I wanted everything from my childhood crush posters on my walls to the tons of Polaroid pictures of teammates and friends on my dresser to remain in place as I settled at school. Of course, I knew I would be creating new experiences at Cheyney University and making new friends, but it provided me some internal relief to know my comfort zone would be undisturbed at home. As they say, "Time flies when you're having fun," and boy did those years in school seem to fly by. Before I knew it, I had formed new friendships, met someone I felt would be my lifelong love, gained basketball teammates, and pledged a sorority. I did not even consider that new things were replacing some old things. It never crossed my mind. Not until years later, when I was moving out and began going through some things my mother had packed away for me, I realized that the once cherished pictures and posters were no longer held in the same regard. As I cleaned out box after box, I would glance at some photos and remember a fond memory. I laughed at some and got angry over a few. I was eerily amazed at the number of emotions I carried years later.

Because I did not have the space or desire to take all the boxes with me, I had to decide what I would keep and what needed to be thrown away. It wasn't as easy as one may think. I felt like I was trashing bits and pieces of my earlier life. I spent hours reminiscing about the good times until I forced myself to get rid of most of it. I didn't know it would be emotional to discard pictures I had with people who had not bothered to keep in touch, but it was. After turning a two-hour project into a few days, I realized I had to turn the page.

The book of Joshua is about God turning the page on the Israelites. Joshua is best known as Moses' second in command, taking over and leading the Israelites into the Promised Land after Moses' death. Joshua is considered a model of military leadership for leading the seven-year journey of the Promised Land. Still, even he had to prepare for the people comfortable with Moses as their leader. Joshua had to have the courage and confidence to be the successor, as he was now the leader.

Disappointment is a tough part of life, and it can keep us stuck in the past. Nostalgia will make you sad about broken promises, shattered dreams, and everything from your past that is not in your present. Being caught up in the memories of what was or what could have been is a hostage mindset that will keep you at a standstill while the years pass by. Learning to turn the page is crucial to having a fruitful life. So, whenever you get depressed about things, know that God has our best interests at heart, and His plan is for us to prosper. Some of the things you long for are just around the corner. Many of the plans you want for your life are still in the story but just in a later chapter. From this day forward, we will be excited about where we are while working on where we are going. We will keep pressing on despite the obstacles, deferred dreams, unexpected circumstances, and doubts. Every day is a new day to continue to write the chapters of our lives, and we will start fresh as we turn the page.

Tamara M. Gordon

What are you holding on to that is holding you back?

_____

_____

_____

_____

_____

_____

_____

_____

_____

_____

_____

_____

_____

_____

_____

_____

_____

What action will you take today to get you to the next chapter of your life?

_____

_____

_____

_____

_____

_____

_____

_____

_____

_____

_____

_____

_____

_____

_____

_____

_____

_____

Tamara M. Gordon

Prayer

Lord, I surrender my disappointments and doubts to you today. Please keep my mind, heart, and soul on the prize and your plans for my life. Today, I am looking for a paradigm shift in my thinking so I can let go of the past and trust you with my future. I know that with your help, I will be all you will have me to be, which is more than good enough. These things I ask in Jesus' name. Amen.

The Making of a Pearl

Matthew 13:45-46

Jesus said, "Again, the kingdom of heaven is like a merchant looking for fine pearls. When he found one of great value, he went away and sold everything he had and bought it.

Matthew 7:6

Give not that which is holy unto the dogs, neither cast ye your pearls before swine, lest they trample them under their feet.

Proverbs 12:16

Fools show their annoyance at once.

Tamara M. Gordon

We can all relate to going through life and finding ourselves irritated at one point or another. Depending on the day we are having, it can be as minor as a missed call or as major as a flat tire. Either way, we find ourselves totally off our square because something happened. Another thing that grinds my gears is having to repeat myself when I know I have made myself clear the first time. I suppose nobody cared last week because I found myself in this exact scenario in professional and personal conversations. I give much thought to something and seldom act impulsively, so I am not easily swayed if I have already taken a position. For the sake of conversation, I will listen, but absent a huge material change or insight, my mind is made up.

With the stresses of life, we may be upset that we can't find our car keys, aggravated that we have an emergency expense with our car or home, or our cell phone is about to die without a charger in sight. However, when these instances pass (as they always do), we should ask, "Lord, what is the lesson in this for me?" Speaking of irritation, people are one of the greatest catalysts. From strangers to the people we love the most, we can find ourselves irritated by something they say, don't say, do, or don't do. Just straight irritated!

The book of Matthew speaks to the Parable of the Pearl. In this short parable, the merchant is searching for the most valuable and beautiful pearl. It is important to note that the merchant was an expert in pearls and would eventually come across one he was willing to sell everything he owned to buy it. To understand where I am going, you first need to know some important things about pearls. Back then, pearls were the most precious gem, even more highly valued than diamonds are today. The merchant is searching the world for beautiful pearls when he finally comes across the one that makes his heart flutter. Understand that this "merchant" auctioned pearls. He already had a lot of other pearls, but he wasn't satisfied. So, he sold them. He was looking for the most exclusive pearl to own.

Pearls are precious because of the process to make them. Pearls are formed when a grain of sand or other hard substance finds its way inside an oyster and becomes trapped. To protect itself from this small irritant, the oyster creates a liquid that surrounds the irritant until it eventually becomes a pearl. This parable is significant for two reasons. One, it demonstrates that the things that irritate us can subsequently become of value, and two, it teaches quality and value are important. Like the merchant, Jesus only wants what is best for you. He doesn't want us to be satisfied with any old gem. He wants us to have the best there is. Further, He wants us to appreciate the process of becoming a pearl.

So, the next time someone is having a not-so-cute conversation without earbuds while you are at the mall, breathe and let it be. When you come out of the store and find someone has parked so close that you can barely squeeze into your vehicle, breathe and let it be. When they get your food order wrong after you've been hungry for hours, breathe and let it be. By learning to embrace the irritation, we can expect something better to come. Every day, we are doing life and playing our part in making our pearl!

Tamara M. Gordon

What are some things that make you irritable?

_____

_____

_____

_____

_____

_____

_____

_____

_____

_____

_____

_____

_____

_____

_____

_____

How can you work on being less irritated so that you may show poise and coolness rather than irritability?

_____

_____

_____

_____

_____

_____

_____

_____

_____

_____

_____

_____

_____

_____

_____

Tamara M. Gordon

Prayer

It's me, Lord, standing in need of prayer. Thank you for everything you have done for me and for not giving me what I deserve. I am asking you to take over my spirit when the spirit of irritability swells up in me. I need you to be the calm amid chaos and to work with my attitude as I deal with others. I know you will help me overcome irritation with triumph, and I thank you in advance for working in me. Amen.

From When to Win

Psalm 21:14

Be strong and take heart and wait for the Lord.

Psalm 27:14

Wait on the LORD: be of good courage, and he shall strengthen thine heart: wait, I say, on the LORD.

Galatians 6:9

Let us not become weary in doing good, for at the proper time we will reap a harvest if we do not give up.

Lamentations 3:25

The Lord is good to those who wait for Him, To the soul who seeks Him.

Habakkuk 2:3

Though it tarry, wait for it; because it will surely come, it will not tarry.

Tamara M. Gordon

*I*t may blow your mind to read that we all spend 45-60 minutes a day waiting for something to happen. Wow, right? Think about it; we wait on our Keurig to brew our coffee at home or wait in line at the barista for our latte. We wait at stop signs and red lights and in line at retailers, the gym, and gas stations. We wait for the postman, and Lord knows we will stalk our Ring cameras for our Amazon delivery. We wait to be seated when dining out and even wait to be entertained. To top all that off, we get up and grind every day, then have to wait for a paycheck. Suffice it to say waiting is a part of the game, and there is no way around it.

Two months ago, I found myself impatiently waiting for my mother to have emergency heart surgery. Never mind the fact that my entire family, including my mom, was in complete shock, but that was just the beginning. She was eventually admitted into the hospital, where we would have tests and wait for the next week. It was a waiting game. Once confirmed that surgery was needed right away, she was on standby for transfer to the main campus, where the Chief of Cardiology would do the surgery. During this waiting period, I tried to keep her spirits high and be a calming force for my dad. We mentally prepared for the surgery, but she was on "hold" even several days after being transferred. My blood pressure was rising because I sat there thinking, "If this is an emergent situation, why are we having to wait?" Come to find out, there were multiple patients needing heart surgery, so we kept waiting.

After days of being unable to eat in preparation for the call, the phone rang, and I heard the lady on the other end of the line say, "Bring Mrs. Manning down." We all looked at each other in silence until it was broken with prayer and a kiss. Five hours later, the surgeon finds me to tell me I can join her in the recovery room in an hour. I am not a hugger, but I could have hugged the doctor because I felt a weight lift off me.

Hours later, I got to see my mommy, but I was not ready. They told me she would be "out of it" but could not have prepared me to see her with the numerous tubes, machines, and monitors with their loud, scary cadence. She did not even know I was there.

Mommy spent several rough days in the ICU, and after she showed signs of recovery, the staff moved her to a cardiovascular unit. I was so happy because this meant she was one step closer to being home, but inside, I thought, *Wow, this is quick.* After two short days in the new unit, she was sent back to the ICU because of serious post-surgical complications. I am still quite traumatized because I was there when it happened, but I thank God for the fast action of the lovely staff who recognized she needed severe medical attention. After another seven days in the ICU, Mommy was then able to be moved. She was still unable to walk and was in a lot of pain, but she could eat and talk in a whisper—none of which she could do before. Even with the best care, her hospital stay was just four days shy of a full month.

I learned a lesson about waiting during this season. I know it is tough, and nobody wants to do it. However, I learned that God is working it out in His perfect plans even when we do not understand. Trying to rush the process can be dangerous, and in my mother's case, it was. Although we wanted her to come home, and as bad as she would have rather been home, it was not for her good to be home at that time. Licensed medical professionals thought she was ready, but God knew she was not.

Waiting on the Lord requires discipline. It also requires

our unwavering trust and confidence in Him. Waiting can be exhausting and even painful, but it builds character and increases our faith. Even with all the surgeries I have had, I learned how to patiently wait and trust in the Lord in my mother's situation.

Have you been praying to God about something for a long time? Are you beginning to doubt it will happen? You see everybody around you appearing to be blessed and are starting to feel forgotten. Trust me on this; you may not see it, but waiting has its rewards. Abraham waited to become the Father of Many Nations. Hannah waited to be blessed with a child. Job waited on the Lord to restore him. Noah waited over a century as he warned people about the flood. Ruth waited with her mother-in-law and later found Boaz. Lastly and most importantly, Jesus Christ is waiting on His Father to fulfill the word with His return. In any event and future situation, I will wait and be of good cheer because I remain confident in the surety and delivery of the Lord.

Write two things that you are waiting for to happen in your life. Include intentional work you are doing to prepare for God's blessing.

_____

_____

_____

_____

_____

_____

_____

_____

_____

_____

_____

_____

_____

_____

_____

_____

_____

Tamara M. Gordon

What do you believe your lesson is during this season?

_____

_____

_____

_____

_____

_____

_____

_____

_____

_____

_____

_____

_____

_____

_____

_____

_____

_____

Prayer

Most gracious and merciful Father, I come before you as humble as I know how—with my heart in your hands and my complete trust in you. Father, I know that you have the answers and are in control of my life, but I am anxious in my flesh. I can't help but wonder where are you. When will you answer my call to you? Forgive me for all my doubts, worries, and fears. Forgive me for my impatience in this season. Forgive me for falling short during this season of waiting. Lord, I need your help to get out of my own head and, more importantly, out of my own way. As I wait, help me to remember that you have kept me up until this present time and that your grace continues to sustain me today. Help me to understand that no matter what, you are in total control and are always working it out for my good. Grant me the comfort of the psalmist in Psalm 130:5 in that if "I wait for the LORD, my soul waits, and in his word, I hope." In Jesus' name, Amen.

All of Us

Exodus 33:18

Moses pleads with God, "Show me thy glory!" And God answers, "I will make all my goodness pass before you and will proclaim before you my name, Yahweh. And I will be gracious to whom I will be gracious and will show mercy to whom I will show mercy."

Psalm 145:9

The Lord is good to all, and his mercy is over all that he has made.

2 Corinthians 9:8

And God is able to make every grace overflow to you, so that in every way, always having everything you need, you may excel in every clever work.

Tamara M. Gordon

*A*t some point in our lives, we have all had something happen to us or for us that somebody somewhere didn't think we deserved. You got the new position at work. You were the benefactor of an inheritance. You got an opportunity to walk through doors that many had been waiting to do for quite a while. The bottom line is that every blessing we receive is given to us through God's grace. In short, God blesses us how He chooses and when He chooses, even though we do not deserve it—none of us.

In 2016, after fifty-two years without a championship in the city, the Cleveland Cavaliers earned their way to the NBA Finals against the Golden State Warriors. While the city was on fire for our back-to-back finals run, we were also traumatized after being eliminated by the same team in 2015. Before we knew it, the Cavaliers were down 3-1 in a 7-game series. Although every media outlet counted us out after game 3, the city of Cleveland dug deep and remained avid fans who continued to bolster our team. As a blue-collar city, we were not afraid of challenging work and cheered our team on in spite of what it looked like. We pulled out a win in game 3 but lost game 4, which put the Warriors up 3-1. The Cavaliers took games 5 and 6, and now even the naysayers were back on the bandwagon. It all came down to game 7 in Oakland, and the Cavaliers—led by homegrown favorite LeBron James—stunned the world and became the 2016 NBA Champs, ending the 52-year curse in sports for the city of Cleveland. After being down and fighting against the odds, there were still people who said the Cavaliers didn't deserve to win. Some blamed injury to players and suspension of others as the rationale, even though they were always factors in physical sports. This is to show you that no matter what you accomplish in life, there will be someone somewhere who does not believe it should be you. Human theory and measurement of worthiness are exciting, but it is God's business.

God is responsible for promotions and promotes who and when He wants. He blessed the Cavaliers with a historic comeback, but He may bless you with a better job, home, income, health, visibility, or opportunity. It may look undoable. People may doubt you, your confidence may be low, and the stakes high, but God still can bless you. You may not be in a big game, but you need God to show up mighty in some areas of your life. God controls what doors open and even the ones that close. He still makes ways out of no way and does not require anything from us. God does all things well and can do abundantly above anything we can even think. We can't earn the favor of God, and we surely can't pay for it. He is just that good that we get to experience blessings because of His unmerited grace and mercy. Not some of us, but all of us. How GREAT is our God!

Name a situation when you thought you had all odds against you, and God brought you out.

_____

_____

_____

_____

_____

_____

Tamara M. Gordon

What will you implement into your life that will show your gratitude to God?

_____

_____

_____

_____

_____

_____

_____

_____

_____

_____

_____

_____

_____

_____

_____

_____

Prayer

Heavenly Father, thank you for blessing me far greater than I deserve. I thank you for your grace in a time when I have fallen short. Thank you for giving me much more than I can even ask for or need—for providing a new opportunity every day to get it right. Lastly, Father, thank you for your Son and the everlasting love you have for me. Amen!

I'm the Woman for the Job

Philippians 4:13
I can do all things through Christ who strengthens me.

1 Thessalonians 5:24
The one who calls you is faithful, and he will do it.

2 Corinthians 9:8
And God is able to make all grace abound to you, so that having all sufficiency in all things at all times, you may abound in every clever work.

Most of us are happy to step up to the plate when the task is easy. However, when the Lord draws us out of our comfort zones and into the unknown, that is when we wrestle with His assignment. From time to time, we have thoughts of what we would like to do, and then we have unrelenting, emotionally driven, and anxious thoughts that God places on our hearts and in our minds with no letup. The former ones we tend to manage a bit better since they are driven by personal wants and appear easier to tackle. Not the same for the visions planted and replayed by God. Those are the ones that make you uncomfortable and require something greater than yourself to accomplish. To make it plain, there is not much you can do to avoid purpose staring you in the face.

For years, I dreamed about being a change agent in an organization of women. I would spend time studying people and learning the "law of the land," with the hope of preparing for a chance that I was never actually going to take. I had conversations with various demographics and began researching how to solve some of the imminent concerns. I learned from webinars, vendors, professionals, mentors, reading materials, you name it! In my mind, I was going to get the necessary data and pass it on to the women on the job. It is important to note that we are referring to years of data collection and innovative strategic thinking. Nine, to be exact.

I remember the day like yesterday when this fleeting thought became a fixed promise. The nulling of the vision no longer showed me as the background but as the woman doing the job. I was shocked, to say the least. My faith today was not my faith of old, but I struggled with accepting this call on my life. I realized it wasn't because I lacked the skills but because I was not sure others would. I spent a great deal of time questioning God's call, and although He obviously did not care, He did not make it easy for me. It wasn't like hearing from God was as simple as tripping over a burning bush—although there have been times when I wish it had been. The short of it is that I became more confident in Him and tested the idea amongst my close inner circles. They were delighted and "down."

As I stepped out there, I kept reminding myself that I did not have to know it all. I only needed to trust God and use what He placed inside me. I did not know all there was to know, but I did know that God makes us complete in every excellent work that aligns with His will. Further, He provides and equips us with whatever is needed to conduct His purpose for our lives. I got scared, afraid, and even wanted to decline God's offer, but He wouldn't let me. Every time doubt crept in, I began to journal and reminded myself what I know God said: *You are the woman for the job!*

You, too, may be struggling with your purpose and wondering how you will get the faith and courage to step in it. I know you wrestle with not being good enough or not having the support you believe is necessary. You may have days where you would rather it be somebody else, but God chose you because you are the woman for the job—the job you are doing now, the one you can do with ease and with no criticism. God wants to move you from it! He says you are bigger than that, and He is calling to elevate you.

You are in perfect company. It is humane for us to feel ill-prepared or not good enough in certain situations. However, if God placed it in you, He would ensure you have everything you need to succeed. Scripture provides evidence of this. Moses had a speech problem but was called to lead the people out of Egypt. David was a murderer and adulterer and still became a great king. God is famous for placing "super" before our "natural" to get the job done. He works through our fearfulness, flaws, unhealthy habits, insecurities, disabilities, and self-doubt.

I hope you are encouraged today and are ready to hear, accept, and commit to your purpose. When God calls you, He will qualify you. No person, group, hater, or enemy can disqualify you. So, even if you have to do it scared, alone, or while kicking and screaming, do it! He doesn't expect perfect; He expects his PURPOSE to prevail. You won't fit in their box. You may not be in their camp. You may not know the who's who. You may not have the experience, education, or credentials on paper, but GOD SAID, "YOU are the woman for the job." Now, go to work!

Write your purpose and determine three things you will do to bring it to pass. Who will hold you accountable?

_____

_____

_____

_____

_____

_____

_____

_____

_____

_____

Tamara M. Gordon

Write down the resources you need and who in your network can assist you in obtaining them.

_____

_____

_____

_____

_____

_____

_____

_____

_____

_____

_____

_____

_____

_____

_____

Prayer

Almighty Father, I know you see me for who I am as my creator. You know my inner thoughts and my earnest prayers. You understand my strengths and weaknesses, and I thank you for loving me still. Lord, help me to accept the assignments you have placed in my life. Give me the total ability to serve you well as I walk in them. You command me to go in confidence and that you will be with me everywhere I go. Help me to live without fear and in the fullness of you. Be my cheerleader when I become doubtful. When things get difficult, as they will, remind me that I am indeed your servant and the woman for the job! Amen.

The Best Gift Exchange Ever

Romans 12:6-8

Having then gifts differing according to the grace that is given to us, let us use them: if prophecy, let us prophesy in proportion to our faith; or ministry, let us use it in our ministering; he who teaches, in teaching; he who exhorts, in exhortation; he who gives, with liberality; he who leads, with diligence; he who shows mercy, with cheerfulness.

Ephesians 2:10

"For we are his workmanship, created in Christ Jesus for good works, which God prepared beforehand, that we should walk in them.

James 1:17

Every good and perfect gift is from above, coming down from the Father of the heavenly lights, who does not change like shifting shadows.

Tamara M. Gordon

*A*s a child, when the doors of the church opened, I was there. My dad had keys to the church, and he did not care if I was sleepy, mad, sick, or whatever. We had to be there. Music lessons, choir practice, Junior Usher Board, Vacation Bible School, Sunday School, afternoon service, special outings, revivals—I had perfect attendance. When I got into my teens, I would try to convince my mother to let me stay home sometimes. This had, at best, a ten percent success rate. Mind you, my introduction to Christ was by my mother, and my dad later joined the band. But when he did, he was all in.

As a young child, I quickly determined what I liked to do in church and what I did well. After years of singing in the choir and being promoted to the Young Adult Choir, I was presented with a coveted invitation to join a singing group. My mother was more excited than I was because all I saw was another evening or Saturday at 4015 E. 140th Street. Now that I think about it, my mother told me that I was asked. I am pretty sure nobody waited on my answer, and this became a "voluntold" endeavor. In any event, I became the group's youngest member, with an opportunity to sing with some of the best vocalists in our church. It was both a scary and exciting adventure for me. I later learned the difference between hobbies and gifts.

Peter 1:4:10 states that God has given all of us gifts. As each has received a gift, use it to serve one another as good stewards of God's varied grace. God entrusts us with certain talents and gifts to build His kingdom. Once we become content with our gift, it minimizes the feeling of insecurity or envy while witnessing the gifts of others. Do not believe one gift is more valued than another; God does not rank our gifts. He is more interested in us using them for His glory. Dismiss

174

the feeling that you have nothing to offer because before you were even born, God knew your life's purpose and how he would use your gifts for Him.

In the Parable of the Talents (Matthew 25:14-30), Jesus encourages us to be ready for His return at all times. In this instance, talent refers to a unit of measurement for silver or gold. Here, the master is entrusting his servants with a measure of his money proportionate to their abilities. The parable explains that the master has three slaves. The first slave is given five talents, the second two talents, and the third is given just one talent. The master advised them all to oversee his money. Upon his return, he learned that the first two slaves traded and returned a profit. Out of fear, the last third slave did nothing with his talent, so he returned just that. The master admonished him, saying he should have invested the money and received a good return for it. This story drives home the notion that when God sees us faithful over a few things, He makes us rulers of many things. (Matthew 25:21)

The Bible says in Romans 12:6-8, "We have different gifts, according to the grace given to each of us. If your gift is prophesying, then prophesy in accordance with your faith; if it is serving, then serve; if it is teaching, then teach; if it is to encourage, then give encouragement; if it is giving, then give generously; if it is to lead, do it diligently; if it is to show mercy, do it cheerfully." With this list, it is clear there is something for all of us to do. God hasn't given us gifts for our own glory. Neither has He given those gifts so we can sit on them. Gifts are to be given away. There will come a time when we will be a benefactor or giver of a gift. Our gifts are meant to bring us closer to fellow humankind and God. Make today the day you unwrap your talent to share with the world in the best gift exchange ever!

Tamara M. Gordon

What is your gift? Do you spend time honing your gift so that you bring God glory?

How will you ensure you are sharing your gift with the world on a regular basis? Who will hold you accountable?

_____

_____

_____

_____

_____

_____

_____

_____

_____

_____

_____

_____

_____

_____

_____

_____

_____

Tamara M. Gordon

Prayer

Father, I want to thank you for the gifts you placed inside me before I was even born. Thank you in advance for giving me the courage and faith to accept my gift and use it for your kingdom. I pray that I remain humble and faithful so that I serve you with my everything. Father, lead me on the path where my gift(s) will make room for me, and I will dwell under your continued grace and mercy. In Jesus' name, Amen.

Lose to Win

Hebrews 6:14

Saying, Surely blessing I will bless thee, and multiplying I will multiply thee.

Deuteronomy 7:13

And he will love you, and bless you, and multiply you; he will also bless the fruit of your body and the fruit of your ground, your grain and your new wine and your oil, the increase of your livestock and the young of your flock, in the land which he swore to your fathers to give you.

Isaiah 43:19

See, I am doing a new thing! Now it springs up; do you not perceive it? I am making a way in the wilderness and streams in the wasteland.

Tamara M. Gordon

*E*very month, I find myself telling a friend or even myself that I am going to get my life together. This is my reminder that I have a ton of things on my "to-do" list and should be making a greater effort to get them done. Suffice it to say that I cannot recall a month in recent years— yes, years—where I have not said this. Sad, but true. In any event, when I sit down and think about what getting my life together entails, it always has me adding more things to do. As if I need another thing, right? Wrong! Seriously, I have tried to understand why I believe that more will get me together. In recent times, I have vowed to rest more, read more, socialize more, give more, and acquire more. I've convinced myself that adding more would magically get me together. That was until today. As I flipped through my journal, I noticed every slot was penciled in with something to do. I immediately felt overwhelmed and had to stop myself from crawling back into bed and accepting another unproductive day.

After a Venti Double Shot Expresso, several replays of Jazmine Sullivan's album, and some sunshine, I approached my calendar with a fresh start. After glaring at the page, it suddenly hit me that I needed to subtract rather than add. This was like an accomplishment in itself because I instantly felt like things were within reach. It took a few times for me to get it right, but after a half hour or so, I had refigured my schedule. In full disclosure, I had no idea what to remove and what should remain. So, I began by asking myself, "Is there anything that does not have to be done today?"

Giving up things reminded me of Lent season, where believers typically give up something to deny themselves in remembrance of Christ's journey to the cross and His resurrection. I began using the same practice on a day-to-day basis. It took some time to get used to, but I kept at it. When I would become anxious, I would say a little prayer and stick with it, reminding myself that little progress was better than no progress. The ultimate witness of addition by subtraction is demonstrated in the crucifixion story. Jesus had one job for coming to Earth—to subtract our sins and make the ultimate sacrifice for us by dying on the cross. Whew! Talk about adding value to our lives by subtracting.

In my life, I have lost people, opportunities, jobs, possessions, hopes, and even dreams, and yes, it discouraged my heart. I could not understand why God would remove things that would hurt me. God has been using subtraction since the beginning of time, and it can be just what you need. Remember, God removes to replace with better. His will is for us to live a life of abundance and not want. Further, with God on our side, we never take a loss. He will bless you with a better job, a better home, better health, better wealth, and surround you with better people if you trust Him completely.

I encourage you to subtract something from your life. Sit down and think about what has your attention and energy and what you can do without. While adding things to our already jam-packed lives is easier, what can you subtract to lighten your load? Fantasia said it best: "Sometimes you have to lose to win." I heard that!

Where are you spending most of your time and attention? Can some things be redirected to put you in a better position?

_____

_____

_____

_____

_____

_____

_____

_____

_____

_____

_____

_____

_____

_____

_____

_____

_____

Has God ever removed something to replace it with better in your life?

_____

_____

_____

_____

_____

_____

_____

_____

_____

_____

_____

_____

_____

_____

_____

_____

_____

Tamara M. Gordon

Prayer

Almighty God, I want to thank you for just being you. Thank you for adding Jesus to my life and allowing Him to subtract my sins to save my soul. Help me subtract things that do not add value to my life or honor you. Lord, wipe my tears when I feel I have lost, and be the lifter of my head when I feel like there is no hope. Place me in the right rooms at the right times and surround me with godly people. Remind me when I get discouraged that you work all things out for my good, and I am being placed in a position to receive better. In Jesus' name, Amen.

You're Bigger!

Psalm 147:3-5
He heals the brokenhearted and binds up their wounds. He determines the number of the stars; he gives all of them their names. Great is our Lord, and abundant in power; his understanding is beyond measure.

Job 37:5
God thunders wondrously with his voice; he does great things that we cannot comprehend.

Matthew 19:26
But Jesus looked at them and said, "With man this is impossible, but with God all things are possible.

Jeremiah 32:17
Ah Lord God! behold, thou hast made the heaven and the earth by thy great power and stretched out arm, and there is nothing too hard for thee.

Tamara M. Gordon

You're bigger than the universe.
You're bigger than the sun and the stars.
You're bigger than the things, oh my, oh my
That can tear me apart.
For I know You're great in all the earth
For I know You're great in all the earth, earth.
You're bigger

~ Jekalyn Carr

*H*ave you ever been in a position where you had done all you knew how to do and did not see a way out, over, or through? How about being in a position where you had exhausted all your earthly resources and were fresh out of everything, including ideas? When we sit and think about all that is happening in this world, we may find ourselves doubting if God will ever show up. I am no different.

I've had more than my fair share of problems too big for me alone to handle. I know how incarceration affects families. I have watched addiction and trauma tear a loved one apart. I've seen someone close to me beg to live and someone else beg to die. While I thank God that I don't look like what I've been through, you name it, I've seen it! Going through life, we have and will continue to encounter some things that we cannot gain control over. It may be a life-changing health battle, a financial burden, or an irreparable relationship. It is in those moments where we should lean into God the most. When our earthly minds cannot work things out, there is only one thing left to do—turn to God. In Jeremiah 32:27, God plainly tells us that nothing is too hard for Him. This passage explains how Israel once again disobeyed God, and they would be taken into captivity by the Babylonians for decades. Yes, the Israelites messed up big time, but even that was not bigger than God!

Next time you're facing something too big to handle, read Ephesians 3:20, which tells us, "God can do exceedingly abundantly above all that we ask or think." This verse will not eliminate major things from happening in our lives, but it will remind us that we can still trust God even when difficult things happen. We can trust God with our fears, problems, insecurities, hang-ups, and even our plans because He is bigger than them all. No matter what things may look like, He has the winning game plan for us amidst times of hurt. God will answer all prayers. God will solve all problems. God will comfort all pain. And God will keep all promises.

What areas in your life do you need God to show Himself to you?

_____

_____

_____

_____

_____

_____

_____

_____

Tamara M. Gordon

_____

_____

_____

_____

_____

_____

_____

_____

_____

_____

_____

_____

_____

_____

_____

_____

_____

Write down your dreams that too big for you but not too big for God.

_____

_____

_____

_____

_____

_____

_____

_____

_____

_____

_____

_____

_____

_____

_____

_____

Tamara M. Gordon

Prayer

Dear Father, you are wonderful. You are awesome, and you are great. Your name is mighty in power. The earth is yours and the fullness thereof. You are the creator of all things, and mighty are the works of your hands. Help me to remember that you are bigger than any financial issue, mental issue, economic issue, and yes, even any health issue. When it feels like everything around me is engulfing me, and I cannot find my way, please comfort me and help me to remember that you are always bigger. Amen.

Because I Said So

Genesis 1:3-4

And God said, "Let there be light"; and there was light. 4 And God saw that the light was good; and God separated the light from the darkness.

Genesis 1:6

Then God said, "Let there be an expanse in the midst of the waters, and let it separate the waters from the waters.

Psalm 50:1

The Mighty One, God, the Lord, has spoken, And summoned the earth from the rising of the sun to its setting.

Ezekiel 12:25

For I the Lord will speak, and whatever word I speak will be performed. It will no longer be delayed, for in your days, O rebellious house, I will speak the word and perform it," declares the Lord God.

Tamara M. Gordon

"*M*ommy, can I sit on the porch for another hour?" My mother's response? "No!" As a child, I hated hearing the phrase "Because I said so." Parents or grandparents would make a statement, and when I would ask why—without an attitude, I might add, the response was almost always the same—*Because I said so.* I don't know if it was the dismissiveness that bothered me, but I do know it meant the topic was not up for debate, and the discussion was over. Period! I'm sure you can relate to a childhood hope or wish being terminated with those four words—*Because I said so.* As an adult, it is now clear to me that this phrase meant to obey what was asked without questioning the authority or needing to know the reason for whatever they told you to do.

When I think about how God directs in the Bible, He is very much a "because I said so" entity. He wants us to trust and obey Him because He always has our best interests at heart. It is in our nature to want to know all the details, but that is not how God works. Having faith means we will trust Him even when it makes no sense and we don't understand. Luke 5:4-5 tells the story of when Jesus told Simon Peter to put the fisher nets into the deep water in order to catch fish. Simon answered, "Master, we've worked hard all night and haven't caught anything. But because you say so, I will let down the nets." It is important to note that Simon Peter is a professional fisherman, so accepting this declaration from Jesus, a carpenter, without question was remarkable. Most professionals would have touted their skillset and presented a case to do things their way, but Simon Peter responded in absolute obedience. And, of course, the results were off the hook. There were enough fish to overflow two boats! Talk about being an overachiever. God is not a half-doer; He does everything in excellence and overflow.

Have a "because I said so" relationship with God. Join the benefactors of Abraham, Job, Sarah, Daniel, the man at the pool of Bethesda, and Lazarus, to name a few. You are in good company. Praise God even when things don't make sense. God has a history of knowing the end while we are in the middle of the journey. Without question, without doubt, and without hesitation, we will trust Him. God said it, so I believe it, and that settles it!

Name something you struggle with and why.

_____

_____

_____

_____

_____

_____

_____

_____

_____

_____

_____

Tamara M. Gordon

How will you maintain a "because I said so" mindset regarding godly directives?

_____

_____

_____

_____

_____

_____

_____

_____

_____

_____

_____

_____

_____

_____

_____

_____

Tamara M. Gordon

Prayer

Lord, I know that I struggle with letting things go, and I believe I know how things ought to go ultimately. You know the correct path for my life. God, please teach me to surrender my complete life to you and help me to increase my faith. Help me to experience the abundance of your love, plans, and goodness for my life. Even if it does not look like it in this moment, remind my heart that you are good and mighty are the works of your hand. All these things I ask in Jesus' name. Amen.

About The Author

$\mathcal{F}$or some time, Tamara thought about creatively writing real-life stories that would merge her values of Christianity, motivation, humor, and authenticity. However, it was the ongoing push by both friends and strangers that sealed the deal. Using her natural wit and infectious personality, Tamara encourages the weak and wounded looking for Jesus and empowers the modern-day Christian woman who knows she is not perfect.

Growing up a preacher's kid (PK), her firsthand account of being in "church" from an early age until now delivers a unique perspective in her book, *High Heels on Gravel*. A finer woman in all that she endeavors to do, Tamara cherishes her family, friends, church home, Cheyney University relationships, sorority, and other affiliations. She states, "A relationship with Christ does not have to be as complicated as some Christians make it. I know firsthand that having God on your side is the real flex because you cannot lose with Him!"

Undeniably gifted as a high-energy motivational speaker, leadership consultant, author, and everything in between, Tamara is the humble powerhouse who touches your life in a way that once you experience her, you are never the same.

www.ingramcontent.com/pod-product-compliance
Lightning Source LLC
Chambersburg PA
CBHW060515130626
46553CB00002B/512